The Future of Nonprofits

The Future of Nonprofits

INNOVATE AND THRIVE
IN THE DIGITAL AGE

David J. Neff
and Randal C. Moss

WILEY

John Wiley & Sons, Inc.

Library of Congress Cataloging-in-Publication Data:
Neff, David J., 1977-
    The future of nonprofits : innovate and thrive in the digital age / David J. Neff, Randal C. Moss.
        p.   cm.
    Includes index.
    ISBN 978-0-470-91335-2 (hardback); ISBN 978-1-118-06381-1 (ebk);
ISBN 978-1-118-06379-8 (ebk); ISBN 978-1-118-06380-4 (ebk)
    1. Nonprofit organizations–Management. 2. Nonprofit organizations–Management–Case studies. I. Moss, Randal C., 1977- II. Title.
    HD62.6.N44   2011
    658'.048—dc22

                                                                                2010052155

Printed in the United States of America
10 9 8 7 6 5 4 3 2

*This book is dedicated to the memory of Michael J. Mitchell
(1946–2009). For decades Mike had a profound impact on the nonprofit
field. His innovative ideas persist decades later in numerous variants
and incarnations throughout the entire industry. He made a subtle yet
indelible mark on the field and this book is our humble attempt to honor
the impact his thinking has made.*

*Mike served as a mentor to countless luminaries in the nonprofit world.
He was revered for his intellect, sense of humor, and personable nature.
Mike's innovative thinking inspired his professional colleagues to
defy conventional thinking and find unique and creative solutions
to challenges that arose.*

*We are dedicating this book to Mike because he had an enduring impact
on our personal and professional growth. He led, challenged, and
inspired us to make a positive impact in everything we did. We mention
Mike often in this book for good reason—the world still has a lot to
learn from him.*

Contents

Acknowledgements

David J. Neff: I would like to thank God for giving me the strength to write this book. I would like to thank both my parents and my sister for always encouraging me to volunteer, donate, and advocate for causes that I care about since I could speak. I want to thank Peter, Barbara, Aaron, Rich, Sarah, and Ehren for giving me time to work on this book for the last year. I want to also thank all the nonprofit people I know for giving me amazing feedback, listening to me, reading my blog, and busting my chops on a daily basis. I hope this book changes the way you work. You can find and follow them on Twitter at #nptech, #npsocial, and #socialmediacrushes. Another big round of thanks to all the social media mavens who shared their thoughts and interviews in this book. And to the man who sent back his interview a week ahead of anyone else, which restored my faith: Rob, you are a friend for life! I want to also thank all the great professors who inspire me and let me talk to their students: Ron, Dave, Tamara, Clay, Dara, Cindy, and Meme. I want to thank the BNF for the most amazing hugs and inspiration in the late stages of writing. I also need to thank Alex, Skip, and Jessica whose time I constantly stole in writing this book. My final thanks would go to Randal C. Moss who never once thought we couldn't do this project, and do it well.

Randal C. Moss: I would like to thank my whole family for teaching me to always strive to make the world a better place in everything that I do. The world could use more parents, aunts, uncles, sisters, cousins, and grandparents like you. Thank you to David J. Neff for everything you have put into this book. I want to thank my wife for teaching me what unconditional love is, and supporting me through every step of this adventure. Writing this book would not have been possible without your constant encouragement. And I want to thank my daughter because her brilliant smile and never-ending laughter gave me inspiration and hope that my effort here can translate into a real impact in her life.

■ ■ ■

Together we would like to thank the staff at Wiley (Jennifer and Susan) who guided us through the process of writing a book in the digital world and then sending it to be printed on paper—and for letting us design a graphic novel to go inside! Thanks to Danny Ingram and all the great staff at the American Cancer Society, and to Dusty Reagan and Beth Kanter for warning us about what we were getting into. Thanks to Nicole for working on the website and Chris for the graphic novel and Sean for editing our videos.

Learn more and engage with us at #thefutureofnpos and www.thefutureofnonprofits.com.

Introduction

We knew when we sat down to write this book that we wanted to deliver both inspiration and tactical advice to everyone who reads it. We knew if we did not inspire and educate at the same time we would be doing our readers a disservice. So, with almost 20 years of nonprofit work between us, and our experiences fresh in our minds, we wanted to write an introduction that would educate you, then ignite you to action.

Don't Crush the Moth

Think of two sets of people. Those that kill the moths they find in their houses and those that try and get them back outside. Now, think of the work involved in those two situations.

In the first scenario, you spot the insect, scream and shout, grab the closest object you have, and swing with all your force to destroy the intruder. Or maybe you scream and shout and signal for help from a fellow member of your household! Either way it's a lot of work with no thinking.

While we still scream and shout when something flies up and lands on our legs, we also have learned to stop, look, and identify. (Unless it's a roach, then we scream for about five minutes and signal our dogs to attack!) Once we identify that it's only a moth that has wandered into our domain, it would be much easier to swat it with our hand and keep moving, but instead some people follow the instinct to help.

In the second scenario, we try and capture the moth in our hands and escort it outside. It seems like it takes more work, but often it does not. When faced with this situation, overall we need to evaluate what to do. What is the moth's life worth? Did it, or could it, benefit others if we keep it alive? How much effort would we expend to kill it versus letting it run free?

Also, what if it was a gorgeous, colorful butterfly? What would the outcome be then?

The same situations hold true for innovation in nonprofits. We are so often caught up in the day-to-day grind of our mission, managing staff and volunteers, and seeking donors and grants, that we tend to ignore things that don't fit in with our paradigm. When an employee suggests we start recycling our aluminum cans we see a butterfly. A gorgeous and simple idea. Recycling? That's easy enough! We can recycle. "What a great and innovative initiative!" the manager says. On top of that she says, "You're in charge of it. Go make it happen." The employee does or doesn't and we move on.

However, when the employee comes to us to question how we enter data into our Constituent Relationship Management system or why we lack services geared toward young adults in our market, the indifferent managers balk and put off the idea. We are all guilty of this at one time or another. This is the moth. It's an ugly and hard-to-understand idea. "Let's wait on that" or "we will add it to our next agenda" are common put-off responses toward change in nonprofits. We tend to crush the ugly bugs. In fact we might get a little secret pleasure from crushing the moths. It's much easier than helping them outside.

You can run the analogy as far as you want. Think of all the flowers a butterfly pollinates during the day. Now think of all the flowers the moth pollinates at night. Now think of the ideas that you squash as moths in any given year at your nonprofit. How many amazing, innovative ideas are you not listening to because they look like moths?

This book is about changing that attitude in your organization. It's about getting the people, volunteers, and structure in place to take amazing ideas and get them where they need to go.

Who We Are

We both grew up in the business world, steeped in digital media, online strategy, and social media marketing in the nonprofit arena. We have more than 20 years of experience creating innovative digital marketing, community building, social media, fundraising, and futuring engagement projects and programs for the likes of The American Cancer Society, The Aids Research Alliance, Planet

Cancer, The Austin Film Society, Best Friends Animal Society, Mobile Loaves and Fishes, Lights. Camera. Help., United Way, Ronald McDonald House of Central Texas, Greenlights, NTEN, Goodwill, and more. Most of that time was spent working together in complimentary roles at The America Cancer Society, the nation's largest volunteer-driven health nonprofit, where one of us was a divisional director of web, film, and interactive strategy (David) and the other served as a national director of the Futuring and Innovation Center (Randy).

Together we were able to collaborate and launch multiple high-impact digital marketing campaigns and engagement projects. Between the two of us we launched more than 15 unique marketing programs, websites, and software and social media projects that drove tens of thousands of constituent engagements and more than $4,000,000 in revenue and, more importantly, our work cultivated a culture of innovation within a 6,000+ employee, national volunteer-based organization. Throughout the course of this book we offer you case studies and insights gained from our real-life successes and failures in driving new products through the innovation-development process.

We have also taken our experience of driving innovation in digital marketing even further by using it in consulting, speaking, and presenting engagements. We have spent time working with for-profit companies such as Johnson and Johnson, MeadWestVaco, *MAKE* magazine, The Alamo Drafthouse, Ridgewood : Ingenious Communications Strategies, and nonprofit organizations helping them all create meaningful digital marketing programs through video and online work. The majority of our work not only ended up teaching our clients how to make the best use of a specific tool or campaign, but also helped them to think innovatively and recognize opportunities. The strongest assets we have given to our clients over the years have been effective marketing and fundraising tools and an ability to innovate and look to the future with a clear strategy.

In part, it is the positive response that we received from our clients after learning how to innovate effectively that is the driving force behind us writing this book. Here, we will give you insights into our own methodologies, and the projects and programs that inspire us. We will give practical and tactical advice on how you can begin and sustain a culture of innovation and, most importantly, show you how innovation pays, how to evaluate the impacts of your innovation efforts, and provide you an approach to sell the concepts within this book to your organization's leadership at both the team level and board level.

Why We Emphasize Social Media

This book presents our current experience in social media and uses it as a lens through which we present our ideas on future thinking and organizational innovation because it is an urgent topic that is relevant now and will be for the foreseeable future. The social media landscape is full of innovative thinkers constantly creating new products and projects. The industry is in a rapid state of growth and development and innovation and new creative ideas are the engine behind that growth.

As with most new media advents, digital social media is having a profound impact on the way that nonprofit organizations and for-profit companies conduct their business. It is both the darling and the bane of old school marketing professionals and executives in all industries because it is such a quickly evolving technology and it has proven difficult to harness its power. However, we are choosing to emphasize social media because of its explosive growth, social and business relevance, and potential impact on the way organizations operate.

Our personal experiences with social media play a substantial part as well. We have seen the transformative power that this technology wields, especially when paired with a business growth strategy that relies heavily on future planning and innovative thinking. We have, through our work with former employers and as consultants, worked through innovation-based activities in an attempt to create effective social media projects that deliver revenue and mission impact.

The current energy and interest in social media is undeniable and we feel there is no better lens through which we can examine innovation. By telling the story of innovation through social media we believe that we will deliver twice the value. Not only will you learn about the fundamentals of creating an organization that can create and drive innovative programs and projects, but you will also get an inside look into social media and how it is driving tactics within the nonprofit space.

However, we also realize that social media is not a vaccine that future-proofs your organization. In fact, within the next five years social media as buzzword will die, and it will become just another way you accomplish your nonprofit business goals. Gone will be the social media consultants and social media vice presidents you see today. The positions will return to what they were five years ago: communications and marketing consultants.

Who This Book Is For

We believe that innovation is a holistic effort to be taken on by every member of the organization. *This book is for every volunteer, staff partner, board member, fund raiser, executive, and everyone in between.* This book is for anyone who is passionate about finding a better way to work and anyone looking for a way to find the right questions to ask and desperate to find the answers.

From our interview with Matt Glazer, Partner at GNI Strategies

Q: Do you have executive support for your efforts?

A: We have to or it won't get done right. If you don't get executive support then there won't be anyone pushing to keep the innovation alive or maintain it once we leave. Having buy-in from the top to the bottom is required for any new outreach efforts to work.

Innovation derives power, value, and utility from the broad-based engagement of every participant in an organization. We understand that to implement an innovation strategy you need support from top executives and the directors on your board. Both of us have had conversations with top-level leadership in a variety of situations and understand the difficulties involved in selling innovation as a business tool and strategy. Innovation as a concept is ethereal and intangible, but in practice it can deliver against business metrics in measurable and meaningful ways.

To successfully drive innovation through an organization, executive buy-in from the top-level leadership is essential. We will take the time in Chapter 1 to explain how innovation can deliver real value to your executives across all their roles. The overall point is that innovation drives real tangible value; the kind of value that executives want to find from any major organizational transformation or culture shift. And as with all major change and process initiatives, leadership must be fully committed to realize the true impact of innovation as an integrated component of the business strategy.

For example, in his book, *The Game Changer*, A.G. Lafley comments on the leadership role necessary to fully realize Proctor and Gamble's drive to integrate innovation: "The P&G experience clearly demonstrates that innovation can be part of a leader's day-to-day routine."[1] Lafley is not just suggesting that the leadership of the company *can* make innovation a part of the daily work, but that innovation is so critical that each leader within P&G *can and should* make innovation a part of their daily work.

From our interview with Holly Ross of NTEN

"Strategically, innovation for the sake of innovation is pointless. Unless you can tie that innovation to your mission and measure your outcomes, it's worthless."

So how would members of your executive leadership potentially see the value of innovation? What are the ways that innovation can tangibly drive the success metrics that are central to their job performance? The answers to these questions are the foundational arguments as to why innovation is a winning strategy for your organization. To sell innovation as a concept at the highest level you must remember that Jeff Immelt, the CEO of General Electric, believed that "innovation without a customer is nonsense, it is not even innovation." In GE's terms, an innovative idea that was not going to drive results such as business efficiencies, a new patent, or increased revenue was not an idea worth pursuing. Innovation

---

[1]A.G. Lafley, *The Game-Changer: How You Can Drive Revenue and Profit Growth with Innovation* (Crown Business: New York, NY, 2008) p. 18.

had to deliver against business metrics, and that is what you need to present to your executives.

What This Book Provides

The bottom line is this book is going to help your organization do more relevant things faster and less expensively, and drive key business metrics. We know this is a tall order to fill, so let us explain the basic value of a well-functioning system that exists within a positive and flourishing culture of innovation.

Proven Methods for Integrating Innovation

This book helps you learn about both organizational innovation and social media. In it, we provide a number of case studies from organizations that are using social media in unique ways to raise money and move their missions. We hope that you glean ideas from the concepts in the case studies and apply them to your organization. What you learn from their success should inspire you to replicate the programs and strive to think of new ways to leverage the technology.

On a much deeper level, this book provides you with a blueprint to recreate the way that your organization fulfills its mission. We are going to teach you the core elements of innovating in the digital age to successfully create a culture of innovation. This book, through narrative, future thinking, and case studies, shows you the importance of each piece of the innovation process and explains why it is important to the overall process, as well as what greater business value it has.

Flexible Implementation Tactics

The book continues to provide incremental value as you implement each progressive piece of our innovation system. We worked to create a flexible process that we think can work in any sized organization. Based on this flexibility, organizations both small and large benefit greatly because innovation is not resource intensive or dependent on a large and available staff.

Each segment of our innovation system can function independently, and you can implement and execute them in any order you please. Each of the segments can and will drive specific value to your organization on its own. However, together, and in order, their individual impact is multiplied and compounded.

Quick and Easy Self-Examination Skills

Building (or rebuilding) an internal culture takes time and should be done in stages. To maximize the impact, we set forth ideas to get your entire organization in a heads-up mode (awareness), create a healthy support system to nurture their ideas (structure), and then help you maximize the human resources you have and find the best additions (staffing). As you read about each segment you will begin to question your own organization's abilities and wonder, "Why aren't we doing this?"

Sparking inquisition is another layer of value. We want you to question and challenge the day-to-day operational norms of your organization. Our expectation is that as you read this book you will explore the potential that exists within your organization and tap the knowledge in this book to help release that potential. Cultural change is difficult, but this book is filled with examples and success stories of organizations that took a difficult look inward and challenged the conventional operational standards of their organizations.

We strongly encourage you to turn a critical eye on yourself to see how you stack up against some of the most forward-thinking organizations and agencies in the country. To assist you, take the quiz in Appendix 2. Use the information you come up with as a preliminary test to gauge the culture of innovation in your organization.

How This Book Is Set Up

When we began writing this book, we saw a great opportunity to not only teach you how to innovate but also to teach you about the rich history of innovation and the little-known value that it drives into our daily lives.

This book is broken up into three parts and is probably best utilized when read from front to back because each part builds upon the part before. Part 1 introduces you to innovation through definitions, examples, and sample strategies; Part 2 takes you through the three pillars of innovation important for organizations of any size; and Part 3 provides you with implementation techniques and chapters on future considerations. Along the way, we offer examples from interviews we've done with innovative leaders at various companies in the nonprofit industry. Most chapters have a detailed interview, but we've also peppered quotes from our interviews throughout chapters to help hit home a concept or two.

Part 1: Definitions and Strategies

In Part 1, we show you examples of what innovation is and what it is not. We introduce you to some of the leading thinkers and practitioners of innovation and show you how they implement innovation in their businesses. The information in Part I will help you to think critically about the way that your organization currently operates. Do your best to use it to identify the challenges that you face, the way you address the future of your organization, and how you handle adversity organization-wide. The more growth opportunities you can identify, the bigger the impact that an innovation program will have on your overall business. Don't be afraid to be critical in your self-assessment. The deeper you dive into your own organization, the greater the change you can make.

In addition, Part 1 also covers the practice of future casting because understanding the future state of your environment is a critical step that helps give innovation activities a framework. Innovation produces the projects and programs that change the course of your organization and future casting sets that course.

After you learn about innovation, we discuss a number of major business practices such as Lean Management, Six Sigma, and Total Quality Management, and illustrate how business models are sometimes detrimental to building a culture of innovation. In the last few decades nonprofit organizations have adopted business management practices from the manufacturing field. We will discuss the value they bring, the challenges they create, and how a comprehensive innovation program can add value above and beyond what these systems can deliver.

Part 2: The Three Pillars of Innovation

Part 2 is all about our innovation process and delivers the tactical advice and specific steps that you can take to create and deliver innovation to your organization and constituents. We discuss in detail the three pillars of innovation (awareness, structure, and staffing), and provide you with case studies of organizations that are successfully implementing the pillars. Each chapter in this part focuses on why we feel the particular pillar is important. We then describe how to address it effectively and explain the value that it can deliver you, both independently and as part of a comprehensive innovation program, challenging you to imagine what your organization would look like if it incorporated the concepts.

Part 3: Implementation and Future Considerations

Once we introduce all of the core elements of an effective innovation program, we bring it all together and show you how we optimally use social media as innovators. We detail how we actively use the core principles in our own work and create our own case study for you to learn from. As part of that learning, we also introduce practical tools that you can implement in your own organization.

We understand that not all organizations have the same access to resources, and want innovation change to be accessible to anyone who takes the time to read this book. To that end, we have included chapters on new fundraising techniques as well as our thoughts on the future of communications.

■ ■ ■

Finally, the Appendices provide additional articles, links, and information to help you discover the power and potential of both innovation and social media. Throughout this book, we give you the resources we use to evaluate innovations with our clients so you can use them as a baseline and then take the extra step to customize them to the specific needs of your organization and get the most value out of them.

Many of the resources used and discussed throughout this book are available at our website at www.thefutureofnonprofits .com. Visit us there to join our mailing list and find information from this book in easy-to-use formats so you can edit them to fit your needs. While there, you will have a backstage pass to read all of the interviews presented in this book in their full and unedited form. We will also release exclusive content, share additional ideas, and answer questions on the site and through outreach we do on the mailing list.

Let's Begin

This book and the examples it provides will be most helpful to you when you start to implement them and move forward toward improving your organization's culture. The book should be the foundation for the case to your team leaders, group executives, and the top board leadership that innovation and futuring needs to be an integrated and essential part of your organization's operations going forward.

Remember: Innovation derives power, value, and utility from the broad-based engagement of every participant in an organization. Continue reading, then begin to implement its strategies wherever possible as soon as you can.

Good luck!

PART

I

DEFINITIONS AND STRATEGIES

CHAPTER 1

Innovate, or Die

The only constant is change.
—Heraclitus, Greek philosopher

The highly acclaimed science fiction writer Isaac Asimov once said, "It is change, continuing change, inevitable change that is the dominant factor in society today. No sensible decision can be made any longer without taking into account not only the world as it is, but the world as it will be." And for the nonprofit world, truer words have not ever been spoken. Asimov had his eyes on society as a whole and his observation was that it was in a perpetual state of change, ever evolving and growing in complexity.

The nonprofit organization is a reflection of a specific segment of society and, therefore, as society and its vast array of segments change, the organizations that are charged with servicing them must change as well.

Change Is Inevitable

To be supremely effective, organizations must actually change and evolve before society and their constituencies change. Yes, the best nonprofits really do change in advance of their core constituencies and in anticipation of the reality that will be the new operating environment. However, that is a very rare thing. This is the paradox that a lot of businesses and nonprofits are not willing to confront.

Every aspect of our current environment is constantly changing. The social, economic, business, health, political, and even entertainment environments evolve on almost a daily basis. For a perfect case study, simply look at the immense change that technology and social media have had on nonprofits and businesses in the last three years.

So if nothing stays the same and everything changes, how are organizations expected to stay current, let alone be ahead of the curve? The answer is creating *future vision* and then unlocking change through innovation.

One of the keys to developing an exceptional culture of innovation is consistently producing projects and programs that *deliver actual value to your constituents* and *deliver on your organization's mission*. Before you begin to deliver innovative programs, you need to consider the environment that you will be operating in over the short term, medium term, and long term. Creating a vision of the potential future environments establishes parameters for innovation and change. The process is commonly called futuring and it's a complementary activity to the overall innovation process.

Futuring for Effective Innovation

Futuring, future scanning, future scans, future casts, future states; these are all terms we use to refer to the act of or the output from a concerted effort to examine the broad environment and make educated guesses as to *what happens next*. When you begin to embrace the fact that your business or organization exists in an environment that is in a teeming state of flux, where millions of variables interact with six billion individual actors, you begin to realize that *there is no one future to plan for*. You literally have to plan for all the futures. (Well, not *all* the futures, but at least for the futures that are most likely to materialize.) Understanding how the manifestation of those future states could impact your business practices provides you the kind of insight you need to effectively innovate.

In an ideal situation your organization is innovating toward a future, or set of futures. Innovation can work in tandem with futuring in two specific ways: (1) Strategy planning for a future state, and (2) agility planning (or proactively working with your staff to create an organization that is able to quickly adapt to changes in the operating environment).

You can leverage futuring to develop a future vision of your organization. The process of futuring is more comprehensive than strategy planning because strategy planning, in many cases, assumes that the current state of the world will hold true into the near future, and encourages you to develop business action plans based on those minimally variant futures. Strategy planning is all about what the organization is going to do, and in most cases it does not consider the environment that you may be doing your work in. We understand that strategic planning may be a tool for effectively plotting the overall direction of a company but strategic planning cannot predict exactly how the business environment and market that you operate in will change and what issues or organizational obstacles will surface in the coming days, weeks, months, or years that will directly impact the effectiveness of an organization's strategic plan.

While strategic planning focuses on the organization and what it is going to do to prepare for what might impact its goals and metrics, futuring can help define the various potential environments that an organization may be operating in. Traditional futuring projects carried out by organizations such as the Institute for The Future (IFTF) or members of the Association of Professional Futurists (APF) focus on specific business topics and create a range of scenarios that may develop based on key factors. Members of the APF have created papers and presentations such as "The Future of Human Health Treatments," "The Future of Electricity Transmission," and "American Television in the Year 2020: Hispanic Influence and Business Opportunities" for clients. Futuring insights help clients prepare for potential shifts and changes in their operating environments. By understanding the potential operating environments, your organization can become flexible, nimble, and prepared to react at the first signs of change.

What is important to keep in mind is that you should not confuse futuring and future casting with contingency planning. Traditionally a contingency plan is something created to provide tactical instructions in the case that a specific event takes place. More often than not, event triggers are catastrophic events that disrupt the organization's or business's ability to conduct business normally (such as when your business experiences a power outage, severe weather, or other unforeseeable event). Interestingly enough, more and more nonprofit organizations are proactively creating financial contingency plans for the scenarios where they do not meet certain levels of fundraising. Unlike contingency planning, which looks at change in a linear "if-then" format, futuring takes a broader look and focuses on understanding the potential positive and negative aspects of a multitude of future states.

In the 1970s, U.S. automobile companies—content with the belief that gasoline was a cheap commodity that was uninterruptible—were delivering automobiles that were large, heavy, and utilized large displacement fuel-inefficient engines. At the same time, Japanese auto companies were producing cars based on the needs of their population and on the belief that gasoline may become a scarce resource. This resulted in more fuel-efficient, smaller Japanese cars and left the U.S. automobile firms at a disadvantage. The United States just didn't consider alternative future scenarios that involved limited supply and high prices (see Figure 1.1).

The 1973 oil embargo had a crippling impact on the economic engine of the United States but it also impacted the way that the country saw transportation. The business environment changed and the automobile companies in the market that could update their production methods quickly to deliver small efficient cars reaped the benefits. Ultimately, organizations that looked forward, considered alternate potential business

Figure 1.1   Fluctuation of Oil Prices

Source: Energy Information Administration, http://en.wikipedia.org/wiki/File:Oil_Prices_1861_2007.svg

environments, and prepared for them found success when circumstances changed. The lesson here is, even if the operating environment does not change, having an organization that is capable of adapting to varying scenarios can provide substantial returns in the long run.

Mathias Crawford from the Institute for The Future puts futuring further into perspective in an interview with *Good* magazine by emphasizing that "...the future is not an end state. Tomorrow will someday be today, which will fade into yesterday. As our world moves through this unyielding passage of time, how people act in our world will determine just which of many possible futures we end up with."[1] Developing a future cast is an event that requires frequent revisiting and evaluating. In his interview, Mathais Crawford goes on to reiterate the point by explaining that, "Even though we can't predict exactly what will happen, we *can* make reasonable assumptions about what potential futures might look like, and in doing so, we can begin to make choices today that can help us bring about the changes we hope to realize in the world."

It is these sets of reasonable assumptions that lend themselves to the creation of an agile organization able to react to a rapidly changing business environment, and help give direction to ongoing proactive innovation activities. Reasonable assumptions, not concrete assertions, are the ultimate goals of a well-designed and well-implemented futuring engagement.

Preparing for Change

Being innovative and opportunistic in any business means being prepared for the future, and planning for the future is something that every business and organization should do. A substantial part of your organization's success is going to rely on your ability to look forward and understand the various social, economic, and mission-related elements that are going to impact your business and your constituents.

As we touched on before, we advocate against creating a contingency plan or even a series of contingency plans, but rather we want you to evaluate a number of macro factors and assess the impacts

---

[1] *Good* magazine website, http://www.good.is/post/what-futurists-actually-do/

and changes those factors may have on your business. Consider if your organization is actively looking at the future. Whether you are paying attention to the future or not, it will occur. (Please see Appendix 2 for a quiz that will help you assess how well your organization is looking into the future.) Unlike a contingency plan that is reactive, futuring and innovation are proactive steps to identify and then create the reality for your organization.

Change is not always a cataclysmic event punctuated by news stories and fanfare. The 2008 financial collapse is a great exception to this rule. The implosion of the real estate market and the domino impact it had on the global economy were covered in depth for months on end. But most change does not happen that way. Most change goes unnoticed and, in fact, creeps up on us. In many situations we accommodate for the change; developing workarounds and alternative processes until that change hits a critical mass. We try our best to avoid acknowledging the change and plow forward, executing the same business plan and using the same tactics that seemed to work, hoping that nothing will alter our output or productivity.

The North American car seat is a perfect example of a workaround developed in an attempt to avoid facing the fact that we are getting fatter. In October 2006, Mark Hogan, president of Magna (Canada's biggest auto parts supplier) was quoted in an article titled "Battle of the Bulge" discussing modern society's obsession with weight-watching. He mentions that this reality may have finally hit the auto world full throttle: "Vehicles are getting bigger because human beings are getting bigger."[2] People are getting bigger in height, width, and weight. However, an entire continent did not wake up one day and become overweight overnight. It took years of slow change, and lots of accommodation, to reach the crisis point. As a point of reference, according to "The Obesity Epidemic in the United States," a 2007 study conducted by Youfa Wang and May A. Beydoun, by 2015, 75 percent of Americans will be classified as overweight[3] and that kind of change takes decades.

These kinds of slow changes can either be a boon for your organization or wreak havoc on it. As a business you have to be

---

[2]http://www.cleanmpg.com/forums/archive/index.php/t-2297.html
[3]http://epirev.oxfordjournals.org/cgi/content/full/mxm007v1

aware of changes taking place and diligently future cast to see what kind of impact it may have on you. But making sweeping changes just before the moment of crisis is not an effective way to maximize the resources your organization has to offer its constituents. Over the last 75 years, the world—and the nonprofit field in particular—has seen major environmental changes that have made substantial impacts on the nonprofit field. These seismic changes sent shock waves through the entire world but had unique impacts on the nonprofit realm. Some were technological, some were social and economic and, in most cases, these massive changes impacted all three areas of society. We simply want to remind you of the past so you can have an appreciation for what may come in the future.

We tend to look at seismic shifts with perfect hindsight. We can evaluate and dissect them for greater understanding but, in our past-tense review, we sometimes lose perspective of the calamity they caused at the time. Even the changes that were gradual and took hold over a long period of time caused extensive upheaval once the impacts of the changes began to impact usual business, social norms, and practices.

If we can embrace the idea that change is constant, we can begin to structure our organizations around that idea. We can THEN create flexible organizations that can identify change while, or even before, it happens. With this knowledge in hand, the organizations we have been involved with have consistently been ahead of the game and reaped the rewards of being the first to move.

Consistency in this endeavor is the key to success and we want to share a few examples of some major shifts that changed our business forever. The following is a case study in how change—slow change—crept up on the nonprofit sector. With perfect hindsight, we can see the slow and methodical change occurring, and almost laugh at the fact that an entire sector missed such a fundamental shift in American society. Consider that at the time this change began, the nonprofit landscape was very well organized and hierarchical. The business model was successful and the roles each individual played were set. Juxtaposed next to ideals of futuring and innovation, the nonprofit field in the 1950s and 1960s looks overly-regimented and restricted.

The Shift that Changed Local Fundraising Forever

In the early part of the twentieth century, direct solicitation was seen as an effective way to raise both revenue and awareness for non-profit organizations. Most organizations had a formal fundraising plan that brought in a steady stream of predictable revenue from households. The premise was to empower supporters to reach out through their personal networks for donations. Programs depended on tight networks consisting primarily of geographic neighborhoods.[4] And the social movement of a post-World War II America enabled this fund-raising tactic. New home development in the suburban areas was creating bedroom communities for veterans. The Levittowns[5] of America were primed for intimate face-to-face, personal fundraising and interaction.

For many years, fundraising programs that relied on neighborhood relationships provided a steady and reliable stream of income. As this kind of program expanded and revenue increased, management structures evolved to support it, spurring the development of local community offices. The geography and proximity of the neighborhood was the driving factor in business development. States were broken into regions and regions were subdivided into city-level units. Sometimes there were even multiple offices to service larger metropolitan and suburban areas. Fundraising grew in tandem with the support structure because at the time it was critically important to have a physical infrastructure to support mission delivery and revenue activities. The neighborhood or city office became the nexus of activity for the organization at a local level and everything flowed through a storefront office or volunteered space.

This model worked and it worked very well for a long time. Large nonprofits grew and expanded their reach, delivering services to many more people in many more communities across the country. And there was one person that was playing a critical role in this strategy: the matriarch of the household. In post-World War II

---

[4]Ideas leverage personal network: http://www.breastcancer.org/about_us/supporters/community_guide/ideas.jsp
[5]https://secure.wikimedia.org/wikipedia/en/wiki/Levittown,_New_York

America, it was typical for moms to have a number of non-earning years. Not just six weeks of maternity leave—but multiple years![6]

Women who stayed home from work served a critical and vital role in the family structure. In an interview with *Mother Jones*, Amelia Tayagi explains that "It used to be that a stay-at-home parent was a sort of safety net—she (and it was usually a 'she') not only took care of the children, but she was there if anyone got sick. Or if Grandma broke a hip, she could step in and provide care without costing the family financially."[7] Beyond being a safety net, the stay-at-home mother was also a social net. She was involved with her community and was connected with the neighbors, and this web of personal relationships is what made her a powerful fundraiser.

As things were fairly steady for a number of years, this localized personal fundraising methodology manifested itself into a number of different programs. Most prominent was the "Notes to Neighbors" campaign, proving that if the person writing the note had enough of a personal connection with the recipient, the solicitor could usually raise money easily from the neighbors. But things began to change in the 1970s. Ever so slowly, the finite neighborhood social mesh began to change and break down. The tight-knit hyper-local networks deteriorated and people began to lose that connection with neighbors. What happened (along with the rise of urban and inner-city communities and apartment living) was more women began to enter the workforce full-time.

When women went into the workforce, they then began to develop and maintain relationships with the people they spent the most time with: their co-workers. The old neighborhood fundraising programs were based on a definition of community that was antiquated by the end of the 1970s. They were programs for communities in terms of geography, not in a changed social context.

Traditionally a "community" was defined as a group of people living in a specific location. When people asked you what community you lived in, they used to be referring to the geography, not the social network. At the same time, the word community refers

---

[6]Citation and research on how many households were dual income in 1950s census data can be found here: http://www.census.gov/prod/www/abs/decennial/1950cenpopv2.html

[7]http://motherjones.com/politics/2004/11/two-income-trap

to a group organized around common values. Today, we know community at its core represents a group of people with a shared level of social cohesion who happen to coexist within a location (be it geographically as in work or a neighborhood but also in places like a community sports team or a digital space city in your favorite video game).

So, slowly and without major fanfare, the definition of community has changed and it changed right under the noses of the nonprofit community. "Community" was a shared location and space where people held common values and organized around common goals. That definition of community was now called "the workplace." As women entered the workplace, they were spending nine hours—give or take—of their day building relationships and friendships outside of their home geography. They were creating bonds and fostering a personal network of influence untied to their street, neighborhood, or even their city. These women were sharing a physical location, common values, and were working together to reach common goals in the workplace. With that demographic shift, the central community place went from the neighborhood to the workplace and it took many nonprofit organizations much too long to recognize the impact of this shift and adjust their fundraising tactics accordingly.

Taking Advantage of Change

When the nonprofit world realized that the central focus of social life was the office, they began to create workplace-based fundraising campaigns. As we said, they realized this change well after it had already taken place but looking at lagging indicators trying to understand why income streams from neighborhoods were drying up, they began to try to supplement the loss of revenue from the neighborhoods by focusing on developing workplace solutions. Some of these workplace solutions relied on the same kind of networked solicitation as the neighborhood programs. In addition, they began to leverage the employer-employee relationship by linking their programs with employer systems such as direct draft from pay checks. From an innovation standpoint, the *population* paradigm shift of the 1970s presented an opportunity not unlike the *technology* paradigm shift we are seeing in the 2000s.

So why did it take so long for nonprofits to recognize such a dramatic shift? One reason it took us so long to recognize the shift is because *we were busy working.* We were busy working at our jobs and executing our individual roles. And while we were working, the world changed ever-so-slowly at a pace perceptible to those who were looking for change but not to those who were preoccupied with matters of daily operations. The operational mindset that organizations hold at the front lines and with their volunteers is based on productivity and execution, therefore, the entire sector missed the early cues: fewer midday bridge games, people walking in the streets on work days, a decline in book clubs. All of which pointed to the fact that there were fewer women in the neighborhood staying home and not working.

Strategic planning is most certainly part of your organization's annual or semiannual activities, but more than likely it is done at the highest executive level. As a sector, we focus our energy on executing programs against our mission and often fail to think about the larger environment in which we operate. More specifically we fail to think about the environmental changes and how they could impact our organization. At the field level, we are missing the chance to evaluate the sociological clues that can tell us a lot about the future state of the environment in which we work. Without insight into the future we are powerless to make the incremental changes to stay on the leading edge of change and risk being overtaken by world-changing advents like women leaving home to work en masse. Throughout this book, though, you will learn that future thinking and innovative ideas are not only activities for the Board of Directors and higher-level executives. Organizations are most effective when they engage every staff member, volunteer, and constituent in an effort to create the most holistic vision of the future and develop programs and projects to make that vision a reality.

From the population shift example, we can learn that change and opportunity are abundant and there are ways we can work, steps we can take, and activities we can participate in to prepare ourselves to take advantage of the next major shift. As an industry, if we look out for the correct factors, we may be able to see the major trends before they have adverse impacts on our business models. If we had been more in tune with the population shift in the 1980s and the future it was going to present us, we may have been able to create innovative programs at the time to take advantage of the new reality. A comprehensive innovation program could have identified the shift as it was beginning and then engaged everyone, including the women who were leaving the home for the office, to contribute ideas toward a solution.

Applying Such a Shift to Today

Taking what we learned from the previous case study, let's shift focus to the current trend of social media. Social media is, by any account, forcing a paradigm shift in the way that nonprofits conduct their business. Not unlike the evolution of women in the workplace, social media as a game-changing technology evolved over a period of years. Organizations that were scanning the business environment in recent years saw the slow and incremental changes in online technology. Their future casts helped to create a vision of how they could engage their constituents and they pressed forward with innovation efforts to deliver on those scenarios. This is why we will use social media as an overarching case study in this book—because it caught so many nonprofits and for-profits unprepared and forced them to change the way they did business, immediately.

Social media is such a powerful change agent that it demanded that the business rules and standard operating procedures be rewritten to accommodate it. It imposed itself on the nonprofit arena quickly and created whole new ways to do, and lose, business. Social media became the catalyst to many great ideas, and the enabler of many bad ones. But like so many major paradigm shifts, we lose perspective as the years pass. Our institutional memories are shortened with each passing year and we forget the technologies and social shifts that previously turned an entire industry on its head. Just like we forgot about the population shift of the 1970s, we will soon forget about life before Facebook and MySpace and Twitter and lose perspective on the scope of change that these technologies brought to our industry.

Yet social media was not the first piece of technology to impact the nonprofit industry. Technology has been creeping up on the nonprofit sector for decades and the emergence of social media is just the most recent. For instance, our institutional memories forget what fundraising, event planning, and advocacy work was like before the fax machine revolutionized the way that nonprofits communicated and marketed to their constituents. Similarly, most of us have no concept of how an organization could have operated without a telephone system. Technologies like the telephone and the fax machine brought tremendous value as they became widely adopted.

Therein lies a historical clue, something we should recognize and remember. When technologies exponentially grow in value with the addition of each new user, they have a major impact on how nonprofit organizations conduct their business. To put this idea into perspective: One person with a fax has no value (you can't fax a document to yourself), but two people with fax machines have value, add in a third and a fourth, and the value grows exponentially. Robert Metcalfe wrote about this very phenomenon and his theory on the value of a technology network—one that links people together being the number of users squared—is now called Metcalfe's Law.

Telephones and fax machines are two pieces of technology that seem to conform to Metcalfe's Law. Each additional member on the network adds exponential value. That is the clue we should have been looking for in the late 1990s and early 2000s as the Internet was becoming more and more mainstream. The telephone revolutionized us. The fax revolutionized us. But fast forward to 2003, seeing how we lived through those massive changes, and it's a wonder how we didn't really leverage the next massive change. We did not properly future cast and got blindsided by the social media revolution.

Social media's mission statement, if it has a mission statement, would most likely be, "To provide the citizens of the world with the opportunity to connect and share their lives actively with each other, to learn from each other, and contribute to the lives of others." Once again we see another shift in community: from geographic to the workplace to online. Even as many nonprofits think of themselves as experts in community, some of us still missed this change. How are we as an industry so late to this party? We were late because we weren't looking at the future and did not develop programs, projects, or the capacity to address and leverage the changes social media would bring to the world.

Texting Donations: An Opportunity Arising from Change

Since we are talking about telephones revolutionizing our communications and the major shift of social media that has recently taken place, let's look at an example of an opportunity that arose between these two shifts: texting.

Encouraging cellular phone-based donation opportunities really began in 2005 and 2006 with CARE and their SMS Short code "4GIVE."[8] But the move to adopt mobile phone donation platforms has been slow. According to a report by USAID, compared to nonprofit organizations (NPOs) in Europe, NPOs in the United States have been slow to adopt mobile donor programs and activist coordination programs.[9] Groups in Russia, Albania, and Poland have been using SMS technology for years because they were in a position where, in some cases, the only technology they had access to was cellular phones and they were highly innovative with the tools they had. If NPOs in the United States were future casting with technology shifts in mind, as well as looking around to see what others in the industry were doing globally, we may have adopted mobile programs much sooner.

Executive Engagement

From the previous examples, we can see how change happens and understand how it significantly impacts an organization that is not paying attention and preparing for what comes next. As we mentioned quickly in the introduction, one of the most important elements of building a culture open to innovation is getting your executives engaged and finding buy-in from your top-level staff.

Each executive sees the world in a different light, though, and your ability to show the value of innovation to a wide range of executives really begins with understanding their business challenges and how innovation may help each of them reach their goals. When reading the rest of this book, it will be good to consider the insight we offer next so you can present the upcoming concepts of innovation

---

[8]http://www.nptimes.com/Jan06/npt0115_1.html
[9]http://www.usaid.gov/locations/europe_eurasia/dem_gov/ngoindex/2009/article2.pdf

to your executive staff and board in terms they will understand and welcome.

- **Your Chief Executive Officer (CEO)/Executive Director (ED):** Your organization has a strategic mission and your CEO/ED is responsible for shaping and delivering on that mission. He or she is working on developing partnerships and creating high-level relationships with other executives so that they can leverage those relationships to move your mission forward.

  Innovation as an approach to business can provide your CEO with a thoughtful, curious, and nimble organization able to make large strategy changes easily. Our approach to innovation, as you will soon find out, focuses on creating a culture of inquiry and exploration from the top of the organization to the bottom, delivering on the promise of an agile and proactive organization. A comprehensive innovation plan could provide your CEO/ED with insights on and solutions to business-changing events that lurk on the five- and 10-year horizons.

- **Your Chief Operating Officer (COO):** Your COOs spend their days making sure that your organization is running like a well-oiled machine. They are responsible for operating your organization in such a manner so you can effectively act on the mission set forth by the CEO and board of directors. Their preoccupations revolve around making sure that the way you conduct your business drives the mission, delivers value to your constituents, and conforms to all of the rules and regulations associated with operating a nonprofit organization.

- **Your Chief Financial Officer (CFO):** At your nonprofit, your CFO or similar financial officer is busy poring over financial records and making projections for your next budget cycle. Your CFO is most likely involved strategically in long-term financial planning and is concerned about the income of the organization as well its long-term sustainability. Every CFO is working to minimize expense and budget properly so they can continue to provide services well into the foreseeable future.

- **Your Chief Mission Officer:** Every day your chief mission officer is striving to drive meaningful programs through your organization. In our opinion the Chief Mission Officer has one of the most innovation-oriented and future-looking jobs at a nonprofit. The most critical thing to remember is that they balance the needs of a number of parties. Because this position is responsible to so many stakeholders, your future or current Chief Mission Officer could benefit the most from innovation as a business strategy.

- **Your Chief Marketing Officer:** Chief Marketing Officer, or Director of Marketing, is a position that we believe every forward-thinking nonprofit should have. Nonprofits of all sizes should have a person engaged in forward-facing marketing, not just a combination development/marketing person. The nonprofit of the future needs both.

  Your Chief Marketing Officer is tasked with identifying your key constituents and developing services for them. They review market research data to better understand those they are trying to serve, and work to align your products and programs with their needs. Understanding your constituents is their main job and their insights are the driving force behind your new products and programs.

- **Your Chief Fundraising Officer:** Without a doubt, your Chief Fundraising Officer or Director of Development is one of the hardest-working members of your executive team.

  Innovation as a business strategy will help your Chief Fundraiser quickly identify new fundraising opportunities wherever they exist. By pulling in ideas from the entire organization, an innovation program can consistently feed new and relevant fund-raising ideas to your Chief Fundraiser. More importantly, a culture of innovation can drive real-time insights from your donors which can help them adjust campaigns, communications, and even invest in new channels.

- **Your Human Resources Director:** Today your Human Resources Director is caught in a precarious balancing act of maintaining the best staff in the right positions through good times and bad. As the needs of your organization drastically shift (to more digital marketing, for example) your long-time staff and skill-set specific workforce won't necessarily be able to deliver on new needs in addition to their existing roles.

As you will learn in this book, part of the innovation process is future casting. Your human resources department should be a central part of these discussions because they will be tasked with finding the staff to fulfill the additional goals in your future organization's mission.

- **Your Board of Directors:** If your Board is like most non-profit boards, it consists of long-time donors, advocates, and volunteers who have dedicated a good portion of their time, energy, and money supporting your cause. They most often have a critical knowledge base and skill set that make them highly valuable advisers.

  Your Board sets the strategic direction of your organization and as a collective has the responsibility to think big about the future of your organization's mission and the environment in which it will need to perform its duties. Your Board most likely gathers once a year for a multi-day conference where they talk strategy, sit in education sessions, and break off into committee meetings for the rest of the year. Your Board is highly educated, very intelligent, and holds strong beliefs about what the best direction is for your organization.

  Innovation can play a role in helping your Board explore the potential strategic opportunities that exist for your organization. As a management technique, innovation can play a role in your annual Board meetings as a way to identify and evaluate long-term trends and business opportunities. Each piece of the innovation process in this book will drive value to your Board, helping them to individually and collectively take broader looks at the larger issues on the horizon.

  One benefit of having a Board that actively participates in innovation is having an extra set of eyes actively looking for new opportunities and environmental changes that can impact an organization's business models. As you'll learn in Part 2, organizational innovation as we define it revolves around the core principles of being more aware of your organization and the environment you work in, having a business structure designed to gather and act on information gathered through awareness activities, and developing staff resources to execute the programs that will move your organization forward.

Conclusion

For too many years the nonprofit industry has been merely reactive. Social, environmental, and economic paradigm shifts have crept up on us and fundamentally changed our business models. In the following chapters, we will introduce you to our formula for innovation and how it can help you predict the future toward taking practical steps on how to implement innovation within your organization.

As we've shown in just a few examples here, change is inevitable, and future casting toward innovation can make the most of that change. Even as you read this book, the environment you are working in today will be different tomorrow. Because of this, we have to ask questions like, "Why are you making plans for tomorrow that only count on the realities of today?" And, "Shouldn't you be taking into account that there could be a variety of possible futures?" These are questions that should be asked at the highest level of your organization. Innovation is more than a process—it is a culture that gets infused into an organization from the top levels and then throughout. Getting your executives and Board to embrace innovation as a valuable tool is a solid first step toward success.

In Chapter 2, we define innovation and offer strategies to help you and your organization not only survive in the future, but *thrive*.

CHAPTER

2

What Is Innovation?

Innovation is 1 percent inspiration and 99 percent perspiration.
—Thomas Edison, American inventor

We have already touched on how important innovation is and what it can do for your business during times of change but we haven't really defined exactly what it is. Dictionary.com defines innovation as something newly introduced, such as a new method or product, and as a verb it means the act of introducing something new such as a method or product.[1] However, we think that's a little limiting. So let's get into the trenches of defining it, shall we?

What Innovation *Is*

In Chapter 1, we referred to innovation as part of a process of change. From an academic standpoint, innovation can be a change in thinking, a tangible product, a creative process, or a tool in the management and structure of organizations.

Joseph Schumpeter was an Austrian economist born in 1883. He set forth a preliminary distinction between invention, which he describes as an *idea executed into being,* and innovation which is an *idea executed and then applied successfully in practice.* The main differentiation between the two is the level of success that innovation

---

[1]http://dictionary.reference.com/browse/innovation

drives over invention. Since Schumpeter was an economist, to him, inventions became innovations when they were applied and delivered the impact they were designed to drive.

Really the ultimate goal of innovation is to bring about change to add value to and improve upon a process, product, or experience. Colloquially, the word "innovation" is often synonymous with the output of a process. However, in terms of innovation, economists tend to focus on the process itself—from the origination of an idea to its transformation into something useful—and its implementation, as well as on the system within which the process of innovation unfolds. Since innovation is also considered a major driver of the economy—especially when it leads to new product categories or increasing productivity—the factors that lead to innovation are also considered to be critical to policy makers. In particular, followers of innovation economics stress using public policy to spur innovation and growth.

In recent years the term innovation has been used as a blanket to cover any iterative improvement in a product, process, or experience. The term, to some degree, has been co-opted and corrupted by advertising agencies that are labeling incremental improvements as innovations. So, in order to understand innovation, it is also wise to look at what innovation *is not*. Understanding the difference will help you better recognize breakthroughs when you see them in your organization.

What Innovation *Is Not*

At the most basic level, things are not innovative when they do not leverage new ideas, new uses for old ideas and technologies, and/or fail to deliver value to the end consumer or constituent. We think that most of what is called innovation these days is not much more than the repackaging of old technology, stale ideas, and product feature developments that truly add little value to the consumer.

In the *Harvard Business Review* (HBR) blog, blogger Umair Haque presents a totally new concept called *unnovation* in his entry, "Is Your Innovation Really Unnovation?"[2] He says, "In the race to innovate, most organizations forget a simple but fundamental economic

---

[2]http://blogs.hbr.org/haque/2009/05/unnovation.html

truth. A new process, product, service, business design, or strategy can *only* be described as an innovation if it results in (or is the result of) authentic, durable economic gains." Umair's description clearly sets forth that innovations can occur in a number of business areas (process, product, service, business design, strategy) but they must deliver financial results. In terms of the nonprofit organization, keep in mind that an economic gain need not be exclusively fund-raising dollars.

Haque goes on to contend that the Hummer, GM automobile financing, and collateralized debt obligations (CDOs) are classic unnovations because they themselves deliver little if any durable value. The Hummer delivers more cup holders and lower gas mileage, the CDO delivered short-term gains and long-term economic crisis, and creative automobile financing is really just an old tactic to sell more cars. Creative financing may give buyers a slightly lower monthly payment, or even expose them to variable interest rates, but what it is not doing is encouraging the manufacturer to make great cars and sustain success in the long term. In general, unnovations tend to sap resources away from what organizations should be doing: Creating ways to deliver on their mission through products and services that are insanely great.

Innovation is not always unnovation, but innovation is also not always the burst of creativity that we associate with invention. Although the terms are often thought to be synonymous, nothing can be further from the truth. Invention and creative moments feed into the innovation process, but they are not always innovation. Remember the axiom attributed to Thomas Edison at the beginning of the chapter? He was one of the greatest innovators of all time.

Pretty Good at Inspiration but Lacking in Perspiration

In another *Harvard Business Review* blog post, blogger Vijay Govindarajan talks about the multiplicative value of a great innovation-development process. Govindarajan's argument is that the innovation process is equally as valuable as the creative content that goes into the process. His research shows that a lot of companies are great at putting creative ideas into the process but their processes are not good at creating innovations from the creative content. The question, therefore, is if you are in a typical organization, where do you direct your energy and efforts? Is it better to improve your creative capacity or execution ability? Improve on your strengths or shore up your weaknesses? Govindarajan found that the average organization is a bit better than average (6/10) at generating creative content, and relatively lousy (1/10) at executing ideas. For an organization to improve its overall innovation effectiveness, he set up a basic mathematical formula.

So which is more effective—moving your creativity score from six (good) to eight (great) or lifting your execution ability score from one (lousy) to three (not very good)? Here's the math using our shorthand:

Scenario	Creativity	Execution Ability	Overall Innovation Effectiveness
Baseline of good creativity and lousy execution	6	1	6
Enhance creativity and maintain lousy execution	8	1	8
Maintain good creativity and enhance execution	6	3	18

It's no contest. Companies tend to focus far more attention on improving the front end of the innovation process: creativity. But the real leverage is in the back end: the ability to execute ideas. Ideas will only get you so far.

From our interview with Wendy Harman, Red Cross USA

Q: What were the obstacles and opportunities discovered in the development process?

A: This is tricky business! There are so many people who have to agree on common solutions for us to move forward. I've been humbled by how enthusiastic all the parties are in looking for the opportunities here but that doesn't mean there aren't challenges. It's easy to talk about this issue but not so easy to take substantive steps forward.

Govindarajan's post hits on the core of this book: The ability to drive innovations into and through your organization is much more valuable than the single brilliant idea. Having a formalized process that helps you get the 99 percent perspiration done right is what truly drives value. Without a concerted effort to establish and grow your innovation development capacity, every brilliant idea that you encounter will be a lost opportunity. It will be an unnovation, unable to increase your business. After reading this book, we want you to very carefully think about your organization's ability to drive product, process, and experience improvements through to execution.

Focus Areas for Innovation

As we mentioned, single ideas are not innovation, and unnovation is not innovation. Innovation is a process, a way of taking ideas and combining them, leveraging them, and driving real lasting value. Innovation, as Haque from the HBR blog explained, can take place in a number of business areas. The rest of this chapter focuses on the areas we believe to be most core to the nonprofit sector: product, process, and experience.

At the Product Level

Every organization is creating tangible products whether they are in the shape of a fundraising event, informational flier, website, handout, or advocacy campaign. Therefore, you should view your outputs as products and treat them like tangible resources that have value.

Your products deliver value to your constituents in one way or another and understanding how that value transfer occurs is important. Often it is something that we overlook. Each year you may do a 'refresh' or a new design of your printed materials to keep the product current and interesting. Your annual gala dinners change themes from year to year to keep a sense of excitement. You develop new advocacy angles and projects for your constituents to engage in. All these things are small improvements usually made year after year but organizations may not be aware of what they are doing or if they are properly evolving to keep pace with the changing needs of their constituents.

Instead of changing the window dressing on your programs, take the opportunity that your constituents give you and work to identify the needs each program fulfills, how successful it is at fulfilling them, and if your constituents are actually content with the program. Connect with your core volunteers and key constituents through personal contact or even a short web survey. Be particular and judicious in the questions that you are asking so you gather the correct information. Most important of all, be open to the comments, criticism, and suggestions you receive because it is exactly that feedback that should drive your project and product decision making.

During the Business Process

Usually, if you ask any colleague why they work a certain way they will tell you it's because they've always done it that way. Believe it or not the structure of your organization impacts how you do the work you do. Internally your organization is structured to work a certain way and, hopefully, it maximizes efficiency and effectiveness. The way the information flows throughout a business fundamentally determines the success of its output. A few examples of innovation in process management are based on challenging the current way of accomplishing business and prioritizing the flow of information and outputs. It involves aligning the employees' tasks with the company's products in a way to best deliver on certain goals.

Toward the End-User's Experience

Experience is the reaction that constituents have when they interact with an organization's products. How do donors feel when they support your nonprofit? How do advocates feel when they sign a petition or recruit a friend to lobby for your cause? The constituent experience is one of the most important metrics and it is often overlooked and undervalued. One of the parts of innovation, as we are defining it in terms of nonprofit organizations, aims at creating a systematic approach to improving the constituent experience. Proper innovation is a way to create unique experiences that delight constituents and amplify the value exchange that happens when they donate, or advocate, or even receive services and assistance.

At its heart, innovation is "creating with a purpose" that maximizes the value exchange that occurs between an organization and its constituents. In short, making donors, volunteers, and those you serve as happy as possible. Innovation begins when you look at your customer and ask, "What makes the constituents happy and delivers value to them?" In order to answer this question, organizations need to do fundamental market research.

Understanding Your Constituents. There is no way of getting around the fact that innovation is going to drive change and, for the most part, you want that change to be welcome. The only way to make sure that you are innovating to the desired goal is to listen intently to your constituents.

Similar to futuring, constituent research is a major part of the innovation pre-process. In conjunction, we would say that the information you synthesize and gather from futuring activities and constituent research is just as valuable to the innovations you will develop. This foundational information sets the stage and provides direction, ensuring that your final programs and products drive mission metrics, help create the desired reality for the organization, and make your constituents happy.

Getting Close to Their Experience. Major innovation firms explicitly talk about the amount of effort and energy they put into research and visioning. Tom Kelley, the general manager of the innovation firm IDEO writes in his book, *The Art of Innovation*, that readers must, "Understand the market, the client, the technology and the perceived constraints of the problem. ...it is important to understand current perceptions."[3] To IDEO, understanding is the first step they take in their innovation process. Next they, "observe real people in real life situations to find out what makes them tick: what confuses them, what they like, what they hate, where they have latent needs not addressed by current products and services."

Surveying your constituents is intuitive, but Kelley is not talking only about focus groups and surveys, he is talking about delving into the lives of the constituents that an organization serves. He is calling for living life with them to truly understand where the opportunities are for your organizations to improve your services,

---

[3]Tom Kelley, *The Art of Innovation*. New York, NY (Currency/Doubleday, 2001), p. 6.

create new systems, and deliver meaningful products to them. All of these goals rely on and come from innovation. Kelley continues by contending that as long as we hold onto our preconceived notions of what our constituents want and how they use our products and services, we will be forever tied to our existing offerings. The existing offerings may get cosmetic facelifts every year or so but they will continue to not quite satisfy the exact needs of the constituents because they have been designed to meet the perceived needs without the research to back it up as time goes by.

Kelley also talks about the importance of getting out into the real world—in the field of interaction—and the authenticity of information that it brings to fulfill the constituents' needs.

Overall, it is important to pay attention to how constituents interact with your organization, but it is even more important to look for the ways they *would like* to interact with your brand—the unfilled needs. It is these empty spaces that can be the starting point for new innovation initiatives. The challenge is that on your surveys and in your field work, your constituents will always tell you that you are doing a fine job, to keep up the good work, and that they are perfectly satisfied if the interactions are too short or superficial. However if you spend enough honest time with them asking the right questions, you can learn exactly where to deliver value if only you had an innovative solution to their unexpressed problems.

Evaluating Your Organization's Metrics. With this concept of delving deep into the constituent experience, think about the resources that you have at your disposal to get it done. We know that some nonprofits are large with upward of 6,000 employees and a vast number of staff in the field, many of which work with constituents on a daily basis. If you work at one of these organizations, consider the learning opportunities to identify those "I wish that…" moments that come along every day. It is possible that your field staff is not actively looking for those moments because they are focused on driving other metrics. Maybe they do not believe that the organization is in a position to act on the information they may find and make changes to satisfy the constituents. Or it could be that your staff are simply not trained or encouraged to collect those types of valuable pieces of information during their regular tasks.

On the other hand, most nonprofits are made up of a skeleton staff, bootstrapping themselves, and trying their best to move their mission with limited-to-no resources. With this in mind we still feel that deeply understanding constituents is critically important to the innovation process. In a smaller organization, everyone from the executive officers to the administrative assistants needs to dedicate some amount of time to embed themselves with the constituents they come in contact with and learn from them. We recognize that being short on staff is a disadvantage and limits your ability to visit with vast numbers of constituents but if you are judicious about the time you spend, and calculate with whom you spend it, it is guaranteed time well spent. And remember, your key donors, most frequent service recipients, and active volunteers may give you that false positive rosy impression, so seek out opportunities to develop the most honest insights, not the most convenient.

One important point not mentioned in Kelley's book (though, we give him a pass ... it was penned before the present online social media explosion) is the advent and popularity of venting likes and dislikes on social media sites. The popularity of sites like Facebook and Twitter has instantaneously improved an organization's capability for delving deeper into the customer experience, no matter their size. So many people are expressing those "I wish that ..." moments every single day online, and not just under their breath, in their journals, or privately with their therapists but out in the open on Twitter, Facebook, on blogs, in chat rooms, in YouTube videos, and on just about every other kind of social media outlet there is. Kelley would probably agree that these unsolicited aspirations and desires of constituents are the most valuable feedback one could hope to be able to mine. It presents the opportunity to unexpectedly delight them with an improved experience. And all of it can be gained by simply searching on these respective networks.

There is no substitute for being as closely connected to your constituents as they are to you. Part of being a first-class innovative organization is the ability to understand the needs and desires of your constituents and develop projects and programs that fill those needs. By creating a culture rooted in anticipating the constituents' needs and fulfilling them, you prove that you hear their concerns, and those concerns are top priority.

Three Innovation Success Stories from the Business World

Sometimes it is helpful to look at and contemplate real examples of product, process, and experience innovation from outside the nonprofit world to fully understand how each is unique. The following three case studies look at how an industrial design firm, an American industrialist, and a digital customer service guru are all driving innovation forward. The case studies exemplify product, process, and experience innovation in action. In each case, we highlight transformative innovation that became the benchmark for the organization; something to aim for on a consistent basis. To be innovative consistently is unbelievably demanding and self-fulfilling simultaneously. One success drives the next, as evidenced by the following three examples.

Product Innovation: The Legend of the Reebok Pump

The Reebok Pump is an excellent case study in how effective product innovation draws on the full resources of an organization. Although the shoe itself is 20 years old, the story of the innovation behind it is iconic and timeless. The entire process perfectly presents the value that each of the core innovation elements (product, process, and experience) brings to an organization, and how they build on each other to deliver exponential value. We like this example because it showcases what a well-managed innovation organization looks like and how it functions. We recognize that not all organizations will be able to dedicate the level of exclusive resources Reebok can toward innovation efforts, but it is meant to help you see what well-processed and executed innovation development looks like in practice.

Paul Litchfield was the project management leader for the Reebok Pump at Continuum (a product design and development company in Massachusetts). Reebok presented Continuum with this customer need: A basketball shoe that could be customized so that the owner could adjust the shoe to fit perfectly on their foot. The solution to the need was based on providing the most effective, adjustable ankle support to accommodate a variety of foot shapes, all within the same shoe size.

The product that Continuum was tasked to make was a shoe with an air bladder support to fit within the design parameters set by Reebok and conforming to the needs of the consumers. The challenge was that there was no precedent for this kind of product in 1989. In an interview at the time with *Sneaker Freaks*, Litchfield explained that Reebok was "looking to make a customizable-fit shoe," and "looked at foams and straps and ended up settling on a Pump mechanism which was hollow so you could change the shape by inflating it." Litchfield went on further to say,

> When we first did the shoes, we just looked at how to make bladders. There weren't many people that made the kind of dynamic air bladders that we wanted. You could do an air mattress that might float around the pool, but that always leaked eventually. We ended working with a medical grade company that made blood bags and intravenous bags and things like that.[4]

After looking at a number of solutions for their air bladders, they found a durable and reliable material to deliver the performance and aesthetics that Reebok wanted: An IV bag material combined with a tongue-based inflation pump. In fact, Continuum even bypassed other designs such as auto-inflating shoes that leveraged kinetic energy from running because their consumer tests showed that users wanted to inflate the bladders before they stepped onto the basketball court. They also knew that the act of pumping was part of the shoe's experience and aimed to make sure it was a central element to the shoe.

But let's take a step back and get a better understanding of how an IV bag ended up as the key component of the Reebok Pump. The team working on the shoe succeeded because they were prepared for success and Continuum as an organization was structured to help them succeed. Think about the staff at Continuum. It is a product design company, constantly investigating new products and development practices. By nature they have to be current on both material and design philosophies. Corporately, Continuum is organized with an exceptional amount of fluidity not only in their physical environment but also in their

---

[4]http://www.sneakerfreaker.com/articles/reebok-pump-desinger-paul-litchfield/

human resources. Structurally their staff and management flow in and out of projects when their expertise are needed and where they can add value.

Furthermore Continuum encourages its employees to problem solve and think of new ways to achieve goals; not to stick with the current way of doing things. This approach of employee empowerment is critical if an organization wants to identify and leverage innovations. The structure of Continuum lends *itself to collaboration* and this is an essential part of leveraging a possible new idea or product.

Process Innovation: Learning from Henry Ford and the Assembly Line

Design firms like IDEO and Continuum are able to succeed and thrive in these roles because they are built as opportunistic organizations. They are ready and able to leverage new ideas and concepts that fulfill identified needs quickly and efficiently. Product design firms present the ideal case studies because they innovate consistently. They are built on the premise that they are not inventing anything new but rather assembling into their products the discoveries and insights of others to make the best possible solution for their customers. This repurposing of existing processes toward innovating industries was exactly Henry Ford's motto. And in the same way that design firms bring together pieces of ideas to create innovative products, your nonprofit organization can bring together ideas and concepts to produce new ways to deliver on your mission, raise funds, and engage your constituents.

Ford Motor Company is traditionally thought of as the inventor of the mass-produced car. But look deeper into the concepts and ideas behind Henry Ford's innovation and you see the ingenious recombination of ideas and techniques that went into producing the automobile in an assembly line process. Henry Ford brought about a myriad of process innovations throughout his tenure as the head of Ford Motor Company. Some innovations were game changing, but most were incremental process improvements designed to make the production of the automobile more efficient and cost effective. This process is now called retooling.[5]

---

[5]www.andrewhargadon.com/Release/Hargadon_Ivey_Retooling.pdf

It is said that the ideas that Henry Ford brought to manu-facturing came from a wide array of industries. The most often referenced inspiration is the disassembly line of the fish-processing industry. Ford took the existing concept of stationed work and a moving conveyor belt and applied it to his automobile production industry. The assembly line in automobile manufacturing was revo-lutionary because its origins drew on existing technologies. These technologies came from the agriculture, meat packing, and bicy-cling industries and were recombined and applied to automobile manufacturing in order to solve customer pain points. Ford was aware of the pain points that existed and to solve them and meet consumer demands, he cut back Ford's two existing work shifts to eight hours instead of nine hours, and added an additional third shift. This idea combined with the process innovations brought together from other industries yielded extraordinary productivity.[6]

What Henry Ford himself says about his innovative nature is telling:

> I invented nothing new. I simply assembled into a car the dis-coveries of other men behind whom were centuries of work... Had I worked fifty or even ten or even five years before, I would have failed. So it is with every new thing. Progress happens when all the factors that make for it are ready... To teach that a comparatively few men are responsible for the greatest forward steps of mankind is the worst sort of nonsense.[7]

The birth of the assembly line occurred at a very important nexus of time, experience, effort, and interest. It took all of these elements to make Ford's innovation happen and the absence of any one of them would have stymied the effort. Ford recognized that he and his cohorts were lucky to be in the right place in history to lever-age the ideas of the past. Without those ideas he would have had nothing to build on. He brought together a team that was steeped in problem solving and manufacturing process. His team brought with them experiences from a wide variety of industries, which they

---

[6]http://www.youtube.com/user/BrightSightGroup#p/u/30/RWwTjxx4WxE
[7]*en.wikipedia.org/wiki/Technology_brokering*

pulled from together in a collaborative effort. And finally there was a strong interest, because for the company to succeed in meeting its customers' needs, it needed to drastically increase the speed at which it produced cars.

Experience Innovation: Comcast and Twitter—Re-Inventing Customer Service

Just as Ford Motor Company drove process innovation, Comcast has been a leader in driving experience innovation in their respective businesses. In the same way that individual products and process can have a transformative impact on a business, we believe that experience can have the same positive impact. Like Henry Ford, Comcast CEO Brian Robertson agrees that the implementation and adoption of others' innovations has had game-changing impacts on their overall business models.

On April 6, 2008, *Tech Crunch* writer Michael Arrington had had enough.[8] His Comcast-provided internet service had been down for multiple days and he was frustrated. After several failed attempts to engage Comcast's traditional customer service phone lines, he vented his displeasure, anger, and overall contempt for the abysmal experience on his Twitter feed. Twenty minutes later he got a phone call from a Comcast executive in Philadelphia asking him how he could help.

What Arrington experienced was an organization proactively looking out for the pain point of its customers. Comcast, unbeknownst to most people, was actually listening to blogs, Tweets, and other social media outlets. At best they were searching for ways to solve the pains of their customers appearing unsolicited in their social media streams. At worst they were disregarding the multiple requests for help coming in through their traditional customer service channels. Nevertheless, Comcast realized that social media was a game-changing technology in that they could do the following: Identify and address those, "I wish that..." moments, resolve customer service issues, and do it publicly for the entire web to see. After getting the call, Arrington remarked in his April 6th post

---

[8]http://techcrunch.com/2008/04/06/comcast-twitter-and-the-chicken-trust-me-i-have-a-point/

on *Tech Crunch:* "Wow, they're doing at least one thing right. Well before most people, they have identified blogs, and particularly Twitter, as an excellent early warning system to flag possible brand implosions."[9]

A year and a half later in October 2009, another *Tech Crunch* article covered the Web 2.0 Summit where Comcast CEO Brian Robertson made this assertion about the impact of the Twitter customer service work. Robertson responded to the general question, stating: "It has changed the culture of our company."[10] Frank Eliason was the original customer service representative (under the name ComcastCares—the official name of the Comcast customer assistance program on Twitter) tasked to monitoring and responding to concerns on Twitter. The article details how Eliason was managing 11 people under him who respond to concerns about Comcast broadcast on Twitter.

What was most intriguing about the article was that Roberts said the conversations being held on Twitter were entirely different than the typical telephone complaints Comcast received.

One reason could be that people approach published conversations differently than private conversations. Published conversations may be more polite and courteous, knowing that the transcript of the exchange may be openly visible to all Twitter followers and possibly repeated in other venues. In addition, people calling a call center expect interaction and a quick resolution to their problem. They demand service and are calling with an expectation which may or may not be met. Conversely, the Twitter response was unexpected, novel, and delivered great value. The online format provided resolution to thousands of "I wish that..." moments unexpectedly. The value delivered was high compounded with the absence of an expectation of service. Comcast was delighting customers because they were filling their needs without them even asking. The cultural shift that Brian Robertson was referring to was that Comcast began to see the opportunities it had to delight its customers, and turned its customer service program from reactive

---

[9]http://techcrunch.com/2008/04/06/comcast-twitter-and-the-chicken-trust-me-i-have-a-point/

[10]http://techcrunch.com/2009/10/20/comcast-twitter-has-changed-the-culture-of-our-company/

to proactive. They began to seek out problems and solve them in a public forum.

Using Twitter as a supply channel for unvarnished customer concerns is now a classic process innovation example. It leveraged an emerging technology to do an existing process (responding to customer complaints) in a completely new way. The innovation of ComcastCares not only drove the core business metrics of customer satisfaction, but created a cultural shift within the company.

Conclusion

Innovation has the power to solve business challenges and re-energize corporate culture. Through examples like Comcast using social media, we now see how there is a real-time window into thousands and thousands of unsolicited comments which can help organizations identify customer service failures, new business ideas, and the unmet needs of their customers.

Comcast did not just fall into the innovation situation we just examined. They were positioned at the intersection of technology and customer need, and had the vision and ability to act on the insight. Innovation is not something that just happens. It is a tedious and deliberate effort made at many levels of an organization.

The main takeaway of these cases can be best illustrated by Andrew Hargadon, Professor of Technology Management at the Graduate School of Management at University of California, Davis, and author of *How Breakthroughs Happen: The Surprising Truth about How Companies Innovate.* He has extensive experience working with organizations to identify effective innovation management practices and says companies like IDEO, and the others we've presented, work well "because people from very different backgrounds are thrown together on a project team. They've each worked in three or four very different industries, so they might have 15 different bodies of knowledge to draw upon. And they are open to talking not just about their solutions, but about their problems and mistakes."[11]

---

[11]http://www.strategy-business.com/media/file/sb37_04404.pdf

The core of Hargadon's message is that organizations that are prepared for innovation innovate, and those that are not, do not. *To be innovative you need to be prepared to innovate.* The core elements of being prepared for innovation are awareness, structure, and staffing. In the following chapters we will provide examples of organizations that succeeded in each of these areas and drove innovation and future casting to benefit themselves and their constituents.

Innovation as Your Strategy for Success

Innovation is the lifeblood of our company. If we don't innovate, we won't grow, or even survive, in today's fast-moving world and highly-competitive business environment.
— Graeme Armstrong, Corporate Director of Research, Development and Innovation at AkzoNobel[1]

There is a plethora of strategies that help organizations in different industries improve themselves. Years of thinking, testing, and refinement have gone into programs that drive efficiency into organizations, and decades of work and continuous improvement have delivered three preeminent programs for driving organizational efficiency that we'll talk about in this chapter: Lean Management, Six Sigma Management, and Total Quality Management. All three are backed by renowned and brilliant economists and businesspeople.

We have interviewed a range of nonprofit people to better understand how these business practices are implemented in real-life situations. There are also case studies and in-depth reviews available that chronicle the positive impacts that these systems have had on a number of industries, and explain the reductions in cost, improvements in bottom line dollars, and lift in quality control.

---

[1]http://www.ninesigma.com/News/NewsView.aspx?id=28

At first, we did not see how the various principles could be applied to the nonprofit field but, as we learned more, we saw the potential value that existed in each approach. We took a look at the nonprofit field and how organizations tend to operate and recognized that, for instance, process improvement and reduction of waste are certainly things that most nonprofit organizations should undertake. In recent years, The American Cancer Society, in an effort to save money, consolidated a number of its business operations into a shared service center. The center currently handles finance processing, travel and expense reporting, supply ordering, and a host of other back-office functions. Certainly this leveraging of efficiency of scale is rooted in manufacturing process management, and it is certainly improving the organization's effectiveness.

Classic business management ethos would say to outsource the noncritical functions to a company that specifically does that function. Check processing and payroll, booking travel, server hosting, even janitorial services are prime examples of where outsourcing yields huge savings due to efficiency of scale. The American Cancer Society, for instance, saw a specific area that could benefit from process improvement and sought to make the most of the cost savings by retaining the services internally. A few good questions to ask when examining the two choices are: While removing those functions from the core of an organization, what else might you lose if you outsource? What are the intangible (immeasurable) benefits of retaining those services? These types of incalculable components rarely play a part in reorganization discussions but we feel that they should, particularly when you consider the potential and untapped value available in each person at an organization.

When looking to improve the processes at your organization, you should also consider the end state of your business. Over the years, we have looked at the impacts of these improvement engagements not in terms of the financial savings, but with a focus on the intangibles that get lost when efficiency is overemphasized. While hyper-efficient manufacturing creates a halo effect, positively impacting business factors like production speed, cost, delivery, and flexibility, it can also eliminate some elements of a company that we think are critical to a strong nonprofit organization: Hyper-efficiency drives out the unstructured time where we used to just talk with our constituents frankly to learn more about them. It decreases the budget flexibility we used to use to address constituent concerns when they arose mid-year. And it also thrives in the absence of the variety that we think drives innovative and creative thinking.

The Three Usual, Large-Scale Business Strategies for Production

Here, we'll examine three popular and frequently implemented management systems: Lean Management (Toyota Production System), Six Sigma, and Total Quality Management (TQM). We will give a little bit of background on each of the systems and then look at what makes them so attractive to businesses. We also offer information about how *we believe they are detrimental to the development and growth of nonprofit organizations.* That's right: We are going to break down some of the most holy management systems around and then offer up innovation as a better solution.

We believe while these systems offer an outstanding structure for organizational management, they fail to offer an outstanding structure for innovation. When we mention the big three, many readers will immediately think of the smoke stacks and assembly lines of manufacturing. But, while these systems may have been born in the industrial growth period of post-World War II, their principles are still being applied across numerous industries today, including the nonprofit industry.

The concept of improved quality through improved production flowed out of statistical thinkers such as Walter A. Shewhart and Edward Deming, and into these systems. TQM, for instance, is an ideal system for tracking down and eliminating variations in production as you push manufacturing and production to deliver a consistently higher-quality product, but the focus is on improving what you already have, not creating new opportunities. Therein lies our main objection to these manufacturing-turned-management systems; that they concentrate effort on improving existing processes/products, not inventing new ones. These systems seek to homogenize production and execution processes, and this especially becomes problematic when dealing with variable, hyper-local, and human intensive products like the ones produced by nonprofits. Next, we look at LEAN (Toyota Production System), Six Sigma, and Total Quality Management (TQM) as methodologies for running an innovative nonprofit organization. While the systems offer an outstanding structure for organizational management, what they fail to do is offer an outstanding structure for innovation.

The finished product and/or output of a nonprofit can be a number of things (i.e., not always a tangible). It can be a special event, a grant to another organization, or a technology or medical breakthrough, and the process by which a nonprofit creates its output varies drastically between organizations and even by project. And, unlike manufacturing, nonprofits make their products with people. Bottom line: Nonprofit work is not neat and tidy like a factory; it is people-driven and can be a bit messy. Because of this, it's useful to review these big three methods and apply some of the ideas, but we believe it is ultimately more necessary for nonprofits to innovate new methods that better fit their business models.

Lean Management

Whether you call it Lean Management, Lean Production, or just plain-old Lean, this system is an amazing and simplistic view of the value creation process and challenges the producer to create only what the customer will pay for, and to produce it as efficiently as possible. Lean grew out of the Toyota Production System, and although it applies to the manufacturing of automobiles, we believe its philosophical approach can be useful and applicable to nonprofit work. As a philosophy championed by Toyota, Lean seeks and strives for continuous improvement and emphasizes respect for people, focusing on the amount of care and attention that everyone collectively must give to the concerns of all stakeholders.[2] These particular ideas fit in perfectly with many mission statements we have seen used in nonprofit organizations over the years. In nonprofits, we strive every day to improve our work together, and take the concerns of everyone we interact with seriously.

But, as we spent a little more time reading up on Lean something else began to catch our attention. It is a minimalist approach to getting work done. It emphasizes cost and effort take-outs and puts a premium on increasing efficiency and improving existing processes

---

[2]Michael Ballé & Freddy Ballé. *The Lean Manager.* Cambridge, MA (Lean Enterprise Institute, 2009).

(something every nonprofit also deems important). However, Lean demands a near fanatical approach to the identification and elimination of waste. It is this attitude toward the overall elimination of waste that we have a problem with because waste, in some respects, is wonderful and we are going to prove it. But not yet. Right now, we want to talk about what happens to an organization that takes Lean practices to the extreme.

When "leaning" out an organization, what you are really doing is narrowing your scope and refocusing your efforts, and the target of your focus is what you already know! Organizations that practice this kind of laser focus can become victims of their own success. They may aim to repeat their successes over and over again and strive to continuously improve on their prior efforts without creating anything entirely new. At the same time, Lean dictates that businesses maintain that laser focus on the known needs of their clients.

In certain industries, focusing only on the known needs of clients is invaluable. I hope that the manufacturing plant that makes bulletproof vests uses Lean. I want them to be really, really good at being bulletproof vest makers. But in terms of nonprofit work, which is multidimensional and fluid, Lean is not as practical. In nonprofits, every day is an entirely new set of scenarios and challenges. For instance, you have to be really, really good at so many things that you end up being really good at multitasking! Multitasking is a skill that we find exceedingly valuable in the global workplace, and we believe it is a skill that is tragically underemphasized by those transitioning out of the nonprofit field.

The takeaway from Lean should be that nonprofits should target training staff members so that they can consistently repeat good fundraising events, advocacy campaigns, and board meetings. That is all well and good. But most of the work done in nonprofit organizations consists of human-driven projects and involves complexities not easily brought in line to suit a production management philosophy. There are no easy ways to address personality problems within a nonprofit committee using Lean. There are no guiding principles on how to produce an event with zero budget (which in our mind is as "lean" as you can get ... and yes, we have been there) and in this way, Lean does not work entirely well in human-intensive organizations like nonprofits.

Six Sigma

Six Sigma is fascinating. The principles behind the process, developed by Motorola, focus on creating high-performance systems by eliminating variability and waste. The goal of Six Sigma is to bring processes into such tight alignment and effectiveness that your organization's process is turning out products that are within customer tolerances 99.9997 percent of the time. In short, your output meets or exceeds customer expectations 99.9997 percent of the time. That 99.9997 percent customer satisfaction corresponds to six standard deviations in statistics.

How is it possible to achieve near-100 percent customer satisfaction? The Six Sigma approach focuses time and energy on evaluating the processes that deliver the end product, and seeks to improve those processes with an eye toward accuracy and elimination of both waste and variation. In a Six Sigma Process, organizations seek to genuinely understand the processes of their production and analyze them to better understand the opportunities for improvement.

Six Sigma was invented to improve manufacturing processes. The purpose was to improve the way that businesses created the goods they were delivering to market. Over time, the Six Sigma process was expanded to other areas of the manufacturing business and improved the effectiveness of other business operations such as purchasing, human resources, and accounting. When we first learned about the wide application of the process we had a difficult time understanding how a manufacturing process improvement system like this could be applicable to other business areas. It was at that point that we did some reading on the production processes involved in the service industry.

Author Kai Yang explains in the introductory chapters of his book *Design for Six Sigma for Service* that there are operational processes involved in every service industry. In restaurants there is a process for greeting guests, seating them, taking and inputting orders, and even cooking food. In phone-based customer service call centers each inbound phone call can be routed through a process to help the customer achieve their goal faster and with a higher rate of satisfaction. But while Six Sigma focuses energy on satisfying the needs of the customer 99.9997 percent of the time, it has one fatal flaw in our eyes in terms of nonprofits. It fails to take into consideration the overwhelmingly vast and diverse needs of the customers who engage nonprofits for similar services.

With manufactured goods, customers have a specific expectation of performance. A car will take me from point A to B and back again reliably and in a certain level of comfort. A frying pan will cook eggs, a flashlight will illuminate the night, and a Nintendo Wii will do all of the amazing things a Wii can do. That being said, we also know when there is failure, that failure is the initiation opportunity to improvement. When the product does not meet the customer's expectations, it has failed, and the product then needs to be made better. In terms of nonprofits, what does a special fundraising event definitively and concretely give a nonprofit customer? Is there a specific feeling or sense of accomplishment that is universal to everyone? With all of our experience in the nonprofit field, the one thing we can say with absolute certainty is that everyone gets something different out of philanthropic participation. To use a systematic approach to homogenize that feeling is a disservice to the volunteers and those you are attempting to serve. To engineer out the variation organization-wide is to engineer out the unique nuances that allow the donors, volunteers, and constituents to call that event or organization theirs. So while there is value in applying principles of Six Sigma and other process-management systems, issues arise in the inherent homogenization these systems provide.

We have had numerous opportunities to work with organizations across the country and in our prior roles we worked or volunteered with small-, medium-, and large-scale events. Both of us have started our own nonprofit organizations and consulted with established organizations. We have organized our own events such as the Austin Tweetup Blood Drive, Nonprofit BarCamp, Social Media Clubs, 501 Tech Club, VideoCamp Texas, and Second Life Community Conference, and the one thing we know is that every event, fundraiser, and project has its own process to get from idea to initiation.

Total Quality Management (TQM)

Total Quality Management is well known as an ideology and the theory behind it is wide sweeping. TQM as an approach has three main components—Just in Time (JIT), Total Quality Control (TQC), and Total Employee Involvement (TEI)—but, overall, can be defined as one that seeks to improve the quality of a final product as well as the means by which that product is produced. In short, if your mousetrap-making plant is running efficiently and effectively, and your process for making mousetraps is optimized, your output will be great mousetraps. At its core, TQM aims to create a consistent level of quality for whatever it is that you are making. The ways that companies have gone about creating that consistent level of quality varies, but for the most part companies are examining their production methodologies, their materials, and their staffs to make sure that all elements of their businesses are operating at peak productivity and effectiveness.

Freedom from defects is the mantra of TQM and, as such, the TQM system aims to empower the line employee to identify defects and act to systematically correct them. Getting the job done right the first time eliminates costs by eliminating the need to redo work. There are numerous cases of businesses employing TQM and it being integral in improving their competitiveness and activities. One such case study from the media industry in India details how they adjusted from being a company with older equipment producing a sub-standard product to implementing fixes and improving their office processes related to turnaround, all by taking part in a comprehensive TQM exercise.[3] The TQM was vital to their staying competitive and viable in such a fast-paced industry. It worked fantastically for their defined and reccurring manufacturing process, something with minimal variation that can be controlled or consistently accounted for.

Another case study we found looked beyond manufacturing and focused on TQM improving the philosophy of an organization. A new financial services company implemented TQM to address the challenges it faced in turning policy proposals into quotes for customers. The process that they were using to research, gain approvals, and finalize quotes was taking too much time and they were losing business.

After exercising TQM principles, they identified the problem, created a solution, and engaged their staff to take on the change needed

---

[3]http://www.isixsigma.com/index.php?option=com_k2&view=item&id=1184: newspaper-aims-to-improve-printing-a-tqm-case-study&Itemid=263

to drive the solution into practice.[4] In this case, the financial services firm looked to internal variables, processed gaps, and focused on the work that explicitly added value. They then set out to homogenize the process across all of the offices and realize those improvements company-wide.

TQM is an ideal system to maintain the status quo at a very consistent level. But as you are well aware, the state of the arena is in constant change and today's status quo is only a moment away from being antiquated. The challenge is that the consistent refinement is nearly the same as unnovation. Making the process work better does not necessarily make the product better.

What Nonprofits Need versus the Big Three Methods

When we dug into the ethos of Lean, Six Sigma, and TQM, we began to notice a few key themes arise: homogenization, elimination of variation, and reduction of complexity. These are all cornerstones to improving efficiency and eliminating waste in manufacturing and production services. If we can get all of our processes refined to simple and standardized templates, we can drive high customer satisfaction by offering a consistent and quick experience. The root to making the organization better is making the organization homogeneous, predictable, and without variation.

It is difficult to translate these systems to nonprofits because they are intentionally not homogeneous. The deliverables, the mechanisms, and the people involved are all in a constant state of flux. In fact, if you look at the industry as a whole, sometimes the biggest product we have is change in people's lives. Talk about a product and audience that is not homogeneous!

As a matter of fact, some larger nationwide nonprofits are legally incorporated in such a way that each local group is individually chartered, which creates lots of opportunity for hyper-local impact and innumerable variations, even though they are all part of the same overarching organization.

---

[4]http://www.isixsigma.com/index.php?option=com_k2&view=item&id=43&Itemid=1&Itemid=1

In the area of organizing the organization of things, management systems can make a positive impact on the business of nonprofits, and particularly nation wide organizations. Preparing community packets and kits, standard operating processes, and donation procedures can certainly minimize repetitive efforts and help in the training of new employees (a common concern that we hear when we talk with managers). Preparation processes can reduce learning curves and help create consistency in how staff members get their business done. All of this leaning and standardizing is fantastic for ensuring consistent preparation on the path to execution, but it leaves out a crucial component in the next phases, especially regarding innovation.

As we explained earlier, innovation is the term we use to describe the small and large advances that take place when people apply new ways of thinking, technology, and methodology to enhance old programs or processes and solve present and future problems. When rules are rigid (standardized by systems like the big three just discussed, say), they do not allow for the creative enhancements or variations that may be beneficial for the organization or its constituents. Sometimes, in the absence of rules, everything is an innovation and a business can actually be in a state of repetitive reinvention.

Beyond the rules and regulations the big three processes offer, the fundamental question for nonprofits quickly becomes, "When will my people have time to experiment and try new approaches if their job and process are regimented?" The answer is that they need to waste more time. (Or maybe, more precisely, they need more time to waste!) And this is where we come back to the idea we mentioned earlier in this chapter about how waste is wonderful.

Time to Think, Create, and Innovate

We truly believe waste is wonderful! To be more precise we think that excess is wonderful. Working companies and organizations into well-tuned machines where every step is calculated, and every worker hour accounted for certainly makes for a predictable and efficient organization, but we believe this kind of extreme optimization increases lost opportunities for creative thinking time and free collaboration. When the only time an improvement occurs is in response to a failure, you know you have an ultra-regimented and lean company. And a system so regimented and measured leaves few opportunities for new idea development, let alone new idea testing and prototyping.

This is why waste can be so wonderful, especially in inventive and human-focused organizations like nonprofits. Maintaining a more fluid work environment and actively promoting free time on the job is what we think helps organizations succeed. There are plenty of companies that encourage their employees to engage in creative projects that are not part of their explicit job description. Google is one such company that is renowned for giving its employees up to 20 percent of their work hours to investigate and create new products and platforms. The Google online social network Orkut and Gmail were some of the most notable outcomes of this program. Although not every one of the innovative ideas to spring from this creative time makes it through the product development process and gets launched, the fact is Google thinks that 20 percent of every employee's day should be a waste of time (with regard to their explicit job description) and it proves how valuable waste is. Google's own website says, "We offer our engineers '20 percent time' so that they are free to work on what they're really passionate about ... Google Suggest, AdSense for Content, and Orkut are among the many products of this perk."[5]

The key words in Google's statement are "work on what they are passionate about." We might think that every employee in the non-profit sector is already working on what they are passionate about, but that may not be exactly the case. For this reason, we need to make a distinction about the difference in being passionate for the organization's mission and being passionate about the job. Your employees may believe heart and soul in your organization's strategic mission (in fact, there is a good chance that they are working for you because of personal experience that engenders their passion) but like most people in the world, they still may only see their job as a means to an end.

The balance in Google's program is that the employees are not exactly working on their job's specific tasks during the "20 percent time" but things related to their work environment; not just personal

---

[5]http://www.google.com/support/jobs/bin/static.py?page=about.html&about=eng

hobbies. For instance, your staff has large ideas and creative ventures they want to try, but because of the way your organization operates, there may be neither time nor resources for them to experiment and implement their ideas. In this case, you simply have to cut out the waste and extra resources that are crucial to the type of innovation Google is exemplifying. Your organization may not be stripped to the bare bones and may not be operating in bootstrap mode, but we wager that if you ask them, every employee's plate is completely full and they are maximizing their time and effort on current and near-term projects. While this is a great plan for execution, it is a myopic plan for growth.

There are many ways that you can drive creativity into your organization and it all begins with giving your staff the time and encouragement to get creative. Take the opportunity to make creative thinking and contributions a performance metric in your annual reviews. Linking compensation to anything is a surefire way to get your staff to execute it. Develop mandatory creative engagements. In one organization we worked with, they brought the entire staff together once a month for lunch during which they watched an inspiring video or presentation from a top-flight conference such as TED, or POP!Tech. They used free resources to get their staff thinking outside of their daily routines.

You can also create problem-solving contests. Take a challenge your organization faces and solicit ideas from your staff. Reward the most practical idea, but also the most outlandish. Reward people for dreaming and thinking big because those ideas can be the spark needed to develop real solutions. (And we'll talk about this more in Chapter 7.)

Innovation as a Strategic Business Tool

With so much emphasis on efficiency, let's take a moment to consider what these process management systems are really impacting. The ideal situation is that the systems make you efficient so you can focus on growth. But what is growth in the nonprofit arena? We understand the needs of your nonprofit organization and know how you define growth. In our eyes, growth comes in a few forms, and, in the nonprofit arena the metrics for growth include income, cost, and revenue.

Income: Indicator for an Organization's Health

To us, income is a top line number. What funds did you raise? We see income growth as a benchmark indicator for the health of an organization and think it is a solid, leading indicator of community engagement effectiveness. So, how can innovation impact income? Good question. Further, how can innovation impact the things that impact revenue? Better question! But the best question is: Can I use innovation to enhance my organization's ability to generate income, reduce cost, and enhance the experiences for my constituents and employees?

Cost: The Impact of Doing versus Not Doing

Simply put, when we talk about cost, we mean the cost of doing business. We are always asking these questions, such as how much are we paying to maintain our CRM database, how much it costs to mail a postcard, and the cost of hiring the right staff.

Most times we do not put enough emphasis on global costs at the front lines. Everyone should have an understanding of global cost structure because that knowledge is what will empower and encourage front line employees to investigate effective innovations that will deliver large-scale organizational efficiency improvements. What we rarely ask is how much a missed opportunity costs. If we want to understand the financial impact of innovation we should consider not only the cost of executing an innovation platform, but also the cost of not implementing one.

Revenue: Improving from Year to Year

Revenue equals your income less your costs. Pretty simple, but the revenue for nonprofits seems to always be zero. Why is that? Well, as nonprofits, quite simply, we need to allocate or spend every dollar that we bring in so that at the end of the year we have no money left. Of course this is an outdated way of thinking and something we hope will change in the next five years. Of course, if there were extra dollars we could find 1,000 ways to spend them in a meaningful, mission-critical way but, it is irresponsible, in our eyes, to not use some type of an accounting mechanism to measure the efficiency of existing programs.

One way innovation can improve a nonprofit's success is in taking a critical look at current performance beyond the annual reports so that an organization's performance can be improved from year to year.

Engagement: The Most Important Metric for Nonprofit Organizations

Considering the big three process management systems in this chapter vis-à-vis a nonprofit's needs, we should add one more factor: engagement. How have organizational transformation systems like Lean, Six Sigma, and TQM impacted income, cost, and revenue growth? Consultants and business professionals can heap case studies onto our desks that show how systems like this have made measurable impacts on businesses around the globe by increasing income through systematic sales approaches and cost-cutting by streamlining production processes, therefore driving up revenue, but engagement is the most important metric for nonprofit organizations.

Engagement is intangible, elusive, and difficult to measure, but you know it when you see it. Engagement emerges in the nuances of thank-you letters, calls from donors, and the amount of effort that you get from volunteers on a day-to-day basis. Engagement is indeed difficult to measure but it is the most important metric for nonprofits. No matter how financially well-positioned your organization is, if it lacks engagement, then it lacks a connection with its core audience as well as a purpose for being. Engagement is not going to necessarily appear on a spreadsheet, but it can easily disappear by way of disillusioned staff members and weary volunteers.

Conclusion

We believe innovation is an overall winning business strategy for nonprofits. We have found in our research that a number of organizations and companies often push innovation to a side department, or make it into an initiative to be run as an ancillary program. In almost all of our research, there were no organizations trying to innovate their way to success in the nonprofit field as we will define it in this book.

A lot of things that might be considered wasteful in other for-profit businesses become opportunities in the nonprofit sector. Every process that takes too long because it involves extra committee member buy-in is a form of waste, but, hopefully, it builds engagement. Every labor-intensive operation that could be outsourced or mechanized but is maintained because it engages hundreds of volunteer hours is an engagement. Each design competition you run that costs more than paying an agency—but brings in hundreds of submissions—builds engagement. Engagement is not lean. Engagement is not hyper-efficient. Engagement is critical, though, and can be a seed for innovation and innovative thinking.

It is because of this that we believe waste provides fertile ground for innovation. We understand that innovation does not appear from thin air and therefore we want to encourage you to proactively push back against efforts to make every process hyper-efficient. It is the areas of managed inefficiency that give rise to new ideas and creative thinking.

Innovation drives a tremendous amount of a business's value. In our search for a previously published systematic approach to using innovation for nonprofit organizational improvement, we came up empty-handed. Simply put, no one had created a way for nonprofit companies to learn about, and eventually leverage, the value that lies within the innovation process.

Over the remainder of this book, we give you the background, cases, and techniques to implement innovation within your nonprofit. These, along with our real-world examples, will help you to recreate and shape your organization so that you are well-positioned to act on innovative ideas and see the results.

In Chapter 4, we will talk about technology and its impact on society. If there has been one key driver of productivity over the last 20 years it has been computing and web technology. Currently we are in an innovation tidal wave of applications and tools that leverage technology and the social nature of man. We dedicate the next chapter to providing you with a primer on the evolution of technology and how it became so ingrained in our lives, and how you can use that omnipresence to move your nonprofit's mission.

CHAPTER

What Is Driving Your Innovation?

TECHNOLOGY, SOCIETY, AND INNOVATION

*The most important reason to continue funding an innovation
effort is that it will keep your organization relevant and in
business.*

—Wendy Harman, Red Cross USA

Think about some of the simplest questions in the world.
Children often ask questions like, "Which came first—the chicken
or the egg?" Questions like this make us laugh as adults but they
also make us think. In this section we will talk about a similar notion
as we ask, "What drives innovation?" Is it technology, society, or something else that drives us to create new solutions? Does innovation push
society to adapt to new technology? Does technology push innovation in the use of that technology? At the end of the day, are we
driving the car or is the car driving us?

In this chapter we will help you come to terms with how technology can be leveraged in your nonprofit. We will work to clarify
how technology can be a resource in innovation and how innovation
can drive new uses of technology.

Technology Driving Innovation

As technologists in the nonprofit world we set to work ten years ago with the idea that technology drives change in organizations large and small. We are fully committed to the idea that technologies improve the way we work and the kind of work that gets done in a nonprofit, and we have a deeply held belief that nonprofit organizations (NPOs) that embrace technology and actively work to integrate it will thrive long term. We came from colleges and universities that taught us the value of technology when it came to research, planning, and communicating. We see technology as a native element of every nonprofit and if a high level of technology integration does not exist, it is one of the first recommendations we make to organizations that we are helping. Great technology integration is a gateway to enabling technology-based innovations. A good example of this is Wendy Harman, manager of Social Media at the Red Cross, who says "the most marked innovation I've been a part of is the one your book is probably about—a shift in organizational culture driven by technology. The social web has given an important role to our stakeholders and we've innovated to embrace that role instead of ignoring, squishing, or otherwise trying to control it. We haven't changed our mission but we're recognizing that technology makes it easier for us to achieve our goals—to connect people and communities to help one another in emergencies."

However, contrary to this idea, we quickly encountered nonprofits that sometimes feared technology and the direction that it was taking. This is a common attitude in nonprofit organizations that have traditionally stayed on very linear paths for the sake of stability and predictability. Luckily, we had internal innovation and technology champions at these organizations that helped us navigate the pitfalls of the nonprofit world and backed us fully in our pursuit of some simple innovation goals. A few common pitfalls we have encountered in nonprofits include:

- The reluctance to make technology investments that are not going to deliver visible impacts to donors and constituents; and
- When a technology investment is suggested, a political squabble arises for control, based on internal power structures and

systems (which are, many times, misaligned with the needs of the constituent).

In the face of these challenges, forward-thinking staff members sit on ideas for fear of seeing the solutions politicized and co-opted. Is your internal structure a hospitable place for new ideas? If not, you may have created a culture that stymies technology innovation even before it gets presented for consideration.

Rallying the Troops

Developing strong mentors and internal advocates for technology innovation is critical to successfully bringing in new technology ideas. One such person is Danny Ingram who is now the Chief Mission Officer for the American Cancer Society (ACS) High Plains Division.

When Danny hired David J. Neff, Danny was the Vice President of Communications. Danny played an integral part in bringing innovation to the American Cancer Society, and served as an advisor to the National Headquarters' Futuring and Innovation Center. He shared his thoughts on technology and innovation at the American Cancer Society in the following interview with David

David: How did the innovation effort get initiated and where/ how do you generate the new ideas and concepts to test?

Danny: This varies. You want to have many different sources or nodes throughout an organization as well as external sources that can feed into this. Ideas come from staff and volunteer leadership, from monitoring trends, from individuals throughout management and on the grassroots level who, through continuous improvement, think of new and better ways of doing things/accomplishing goals.

David: Do you have executive support for your efforts? How is your role/department structured?

Danny: Yes, it's a stated part of my job responsibilities which comes directly from the CEO. It's only one part, but it allows for seeing anything from big picture, global implications to community-based implications. Innovation requires experimenting, failing, re-directing, trying again, adjusting, tweaking, and learning from it.

David: What are your requirements before you invest time and money into a new project?

Danny: We have a "stage/gate" innovation process that helps manage bottom-up and top-down efforts, evaluates them at each stage in order to determine if we move forward to the next stage, and eventually determines if we need to invest funds for testing to prove the concept before getting to a final determination of whether or not the project meets the intended needs and is implemented. Overlay this with return on investment (ROI) to mission and organizational efficiencies and effectiveness. A goal is to have a diversified portfolio of innovation projects in the pipeline at all times.

David: What is the most valuable thing you have learned both tactically and strategically?

Danny: The "champion" for the project is key for organizational navigation and buy-in; additionally, being open-minded and patient is important.

■ ■ ■

One line we really love from this interview is that, "A goal is to have a diversified portfolio of innovation projects in the pipeline at all times." Ingram is stating that not just one project at a time is rocketing through the stages/gates but several projects are all working their way through the development and prototype process simultaneously. What is particularly advantageous about this system of continual project work is that it provides each new project with the opportunity to learn from all of the other projects, incorporate their technological advances, and, in the end, every prototype benefited from the others. The other line we really took notice of from the interview is, "Yes, it's a *stated part of my job responsibilities which comes directly from the CEO*. It's only one part, but it allows for seeing anything from big picture, global implications to community-based implications." This is a very important part of the structure and staffing of innovation programs and one which we will cover in later chapters of the book.

Similar to how design firms like IDEO and Design Continuum are able to reuse technology to drive multiple projects, the innovation center at the ACS was able to reuse technology concepts and lessons to shorten development cycles and reduce costs.

Example: SharingHope.TV

The process described by Danny at the American Cancer Society is interesting and one that David experienced first-hand when creating SharingHope.TV in 2008. SharingHope.TV was the nonprofit world's first user-generated content website for people affected by cancer and their supporters. He presented the concept and business plan to the American Cancer Society's Futuring and Innovation Center and requested $20,000 in initial funding to develop the idea into a reality.

At the same time David pitched SharingHope.TV, the Futuring and Innovation Center was also prototyping a virtual office in the world of Second Life. Second Life is a free three-dimensional virtual world where users can socialize, connect, and create using free voice and text chat.[1] The Innovation Center at the ACS was also simultaneously supporting the development of new fundraising technology solutions for athletic events in conjunction with the New York regional office and a digital health reminder assistant in collaboration with the Seattle regional office. Together, all of these projects flowed into one another, competed for attention, and drove a community of innovation around technology.

Because of this, in the building of SharingHope.TV, David looked outside the technology walls of the American Cancer Society for help. In what was, at the time, a mostly Microsoft.ASP-dominated technology shop nonprofits, David chose to build SharingHope.TV on the programming languages of PHP and Ruby on Rails. Building the site on these frameworks with local Texas talent helped reduce costs and timelines. In addition, this project marked the first time that the ACS leveraged an outside API (Application Programming Interface). SharingHope.TV was built on the VMIX API, and the American Cancer Society leveraged the VMIX API library to add online video, photo, audio, and community-building tools to the

---

[1]http://secondlife.com/whatis

website. VMIX APIs enabled ACS to access media in users' libraries (user-generated content) and featured interactive elements like comments and ratings. This enabled users to upload their own content as well as allowing other users to add them as friends, favorite their works, and leave public-facing comments on their stories. Without the use of an API to power this network of content, it would have cost thousands of dollars more to implement such robust community elements.

In this particular case, technology (readily available video combined with text and low-cost cameras) drove innovation. Five years before this technology hit the marketplace, it would have been nearly impossible to let cancer patients get online and share, much less through videos and photos.

Raising Funds in the Virtual World

Similarly in the case of Second Life, the advent of higher-powered computer processors and video cards drove innovation in online video games. These video game engines combined with the connectivity of the Internet gave birth to three-dimensional virtual worlds where individuals were able to create their own communities. The combination of rich graphics, VoIP (Voice over Internet Protocol), and streaming media made the online virtual world a rich and engaging online environment in which users developed complex and meaningful relationships with each other and with the space.

As evident in the virtual world space, in order to create deep and connecting user experiences, it is often necessary to find new technologies. Many times there are solutions already in existence to drive the desired outcomes—whether it is the ability to vote on content, send instant messages between users, or share multimedia. The challenge most nonprofits have, though, is having the insight to know when they need to invest in external systems, or initiate additional development work internally.

Randy experienced this challenge firsthand when he was developing and launching the Second Life initiative to raise funds and awareness for the American Cancer Society. The technology of Second Life was completely foreign to the American Cancer Society and every other nonprofit. The leverage of a completely digital virtual community was beyond their technological expertise, but the business plan presented to the Innovation Center made a case for using existing fundraising methods to support innovation in this new space. The Second Life events required the use of outside technologies and forced the development of new business practices. Part of the justification for the workarounds and technology investments was the potential income from the new venture. The Second Life venture was not an experiment for technology's sake, but rather a sound investment into a new way of doing business that has generated more than $800,000 since its inception in 2005.

IT versus the Rest of Us, or "Did You Turn It Off and Then On Again?"

As innovators who enjoy using internet technology it pains us to pile added work on the friends and family of ours that are information technology (IT) professionals. After all, these are the folks who are working hard to maintain your network and keep your website up. When innovation comes up in conversation we fail to fully consider the implications of our requests beyond what we read in a magazine, or see on TV, assuming that, yes, it really is *that* easy to do. You never really appreciate the IT people until something goes wrong and most nonprofits treat IT as a support/overhead function whereas an exceptional IT infrastructure and development team can help an organization be better organized, run more efficiently, raise more dollars, and deliver on their mission more efficiently. This is why you traditionally get so much pushback from IT. You do not consider the needs or implications on their work when you decide to launch the next innovative digital initiative. No wonder the relationship between IT and innovators always seems a bit strained!

We believe that there would be no war at all if there was more education and cooperation between the IT/tech folks at nonprofits and the mission programming and fundraising folks, but fear is a big issue. A common scenario is that programming staff at nonprofits are scared to approach IT with their ideas and IT staff are afraid of changing the way they have always done things. Mission folks then keep their ideas to themselves so that once the executives see them, IT will be forced into conforming to their plan, even if there were a better way to do things. Your IT staff ends up feeling like those on the mission side constantly avoid talking with them while programs are in development. And since they feel out of the loop they are less inclined to help once projects have been approved and forced upon them.

There is a simple solution to these situations: Talk to them. Every innovation project we have ever completed with an organization included an IT person as a core member of the business review and development team. You would be surprised at how flexible they can be when they feel like they have ownership of a project. The best part about engaging the technical team in advance is that you can leverage their knowledge of internal systems and external advancements to make the most of a proposed idea. Most importantly they can help create an internal sales strategy to help you sell your technology innovation to executives for support. It is actually a large part of what they do overall. They often sell executives on spending money on technology projects. Learn a lesson from them on how to present your innovation programs and include them in the implementation.

As John Kenyon, a nonprofit Technology Educator & Strategist, told us: "Through my practice I have seen that many people have a fear of technology. They did not grow up using it or they are not comfortable with it or maybe it is just not their strong suit. Just last month I had the Executive Director at a client start our first meeting by saying 'I am a dinosaur—I don't have a computer at home and I don't get any of this Facebook or Twitter stuff.' So the fear and lack of enthusiasm still exists."[2]

He also goes on to say, "The communication issue I mention here also seems to get in the way of program, line, and management staff communicating effectively with software programmers and vice-versa." In general, the nonprofit staff that is driving innovation through technology often runs into problems with two main things, IT intervention and unclear communications.

An IT Intervention. GNI Strategies is an integrated political consulting firm that provides new media analysis and general consulting. Matt Glazer, a partner in GNI Strategies, has a lot of good insights about helping nonprofits. There is a tremendous change in communications happening. Tons of nonprofits are starting to use

---

[2]Interview via email.

new tools to do everything from donations to tracking return on investment (ROI). Matt says, "The familiarity with new media and social networking has skyrocketed since 2008, but the knowledge and time for nonprofits to effectively leverage these new resources hasn't caught up with the will to implement the tools."[3] So in the case of anything relating to social media from geo-location to video downloads, it can be hard for nonprofit IT staff to handle the rapid changes because they have not been given the resources necessary to develop, integrate, and implement the tools or dependable support structures for them.

So let's pile a little more on their plates. To quote Dave McClure of 500 Hats, "... the consumer Internet has brought a tsunami of technological and behavioral change which has resulted in stunning reductions in time and cost needed to distribute products and services to the over 2-3B connected people on the planet."[4] It's essentially a tsunami of technical change washing up onto our legacy systems and we expect that since we see technologists and startups lauding these applications as "easy to use" and "simple to integrate," we assume they are talking about our legacy systems, too, right? Not so much!

In the nonprofit world we tend to use our technology systems as long as we can, often long past the point of technological obsolescence. That does not mean our systems are functionally obsolete; they work just fine. Our databases still have data, and we can still search that data. Our fundraising platform still collects money and gives receipts to the folks who donate on our website with a credit card. However our systems lack the technical flexibility to integrate with the new systems of today and that engenders frustration and impacts everything from fundraising to acquiring new donors.

We know that, as nonprofits, you are not going to migrate your entire database system to a "new" version that you know will be an "old" version by the time the migration is done. You are not going to make the large capital investments for state-of-the-art systems, but instead use your funds to deliver on your mission directly. You are afraid of investing because you believe that your purchase will

---

[3]Interview via email.
[4]http://500hats.typepad.com/500blogs/2010/07/moneyball-for-startups.html

be out-of-date in three months. Moreover, your board will never approve that expense based on the need for it to "play nice with Facebook."

Your fear is real and rational, but misplaced. What you are looking at is a single system at a tactical level instead of your strategic technology plan as a whole. Replacing one system to play well with social media is not prudent, but replacing all of your systems to play nicely with each other, and outside systems, is a valuable strategy. In Chapter 5 we will talk about being aware of the environment in which you operate, and this is a perfect example of why it is important to understand the ever-changing technical environment.

If you are not the individual keeping tabs on the technology sector, make sure your IT person is, and then pay attention to what they are saying! You are in this aggravating predicament of old legacy equipment because you did not pay enough attention to the right strategic things and then tasked your best human asset to running your servers, fixing the dodgy keyboard for the administrative assistant, and explaining to your executive director why he can't download The Beatles to put in his keynote presentation.

You can start to understand where the challenge is for people using technology in innovative ways. They are often doing things that IT staff simply doesn't understand. A lot of times it is because they don't have time to understand but, more importantly, it's that they don't get paid to understand. This is a major deficiency in most organizations.

IT in nonprofits is thrown into the back office and called on when needed. Then nonprofits complain when IT staff don't know anything about the mission or are reluctant to support change. There is one nonprofit that we are totally in awe of that is working to change this for all other nonprofits: the Nonprofit Technology Education Network (NTEN). NTEN was created specifically to change this model we've been describing. Holly Ross, NTEN Executive Director, had this to say about its Technology Leadership Academy (The Academy brings together 100 participants from 50 nonprofit organizations for a nine-week online training program designed to create nonprofit technology leaders) where IT staff enroll to change the nonprofit world: "Our Technology Leadership Academy is another example of innovation in attitude, although for a long time, we would not have been able to articulate it that way . . . . . . It's funny, but just saying that technology is central to our ability to meet our missions has been viewed as pretty audacious."[5]

That's part of the problem, right? She goes on to say, "The Academy is also innovative in its approach. We don't believe that you can address technology in your organization without also delving into other management disciplines like change management and human resources. Because technology doesn't happen in a silo, we can't teach people how to use it effectively in a silo."

So go take a look at your nonprofit IT staff (if you have them) and make sure they understand what the whole organization is really trying to accomplish. And then do them a favor and get the whole organization to understand the IT staff. And if you haven't already, get the Executive Director and IT staff enrolled in the NTEN Leadership Academy.

Ending Unclear Communications. A major sticking point with IT/tech staff is that nonprofit program people are not speaking their language and they are not speaking yours. If you reflect on what you've read so far in this chapter and the issues that we highlight, we think you would agree you see this trend in your nonprofit. That's not a good thing. John Kenyon brought up such an example in our interview with him by stating, "I was working with a group of programmers on a database tool that was primarily used in the United States. When they created a pull-down menu of countries, they listed them all alphabetically, putting the U.S. near the bottom of a list of hundreds of countries. I was surprised that I had to explain to the programmers that it would save their users a lot of unnecessary effort and time scrolling down that list every time they entered a record, putting the U.S. at the top of that list might make better sense." However, he goes on to say, "I have seen nonprofit staff doing a terrible job communicating what they want not only to programmers but to graphic designers as well. 'I want it better' is not constructive feedback on a design."

The cure for all these problems, and the way the nonprofit of the future will think, is that mission comes before technology

---

[5]Interview via email.

always, but that *technology needs a seat at the leadership table*. If you're not doing this at your nonprofit today then you are already out of touch with the current reality and falling behind the emerging economy.

Example: The Brooklyn Museum

Our good friend and fellow author Beth Kanter introduced us to a great example of technology driving innovative change at the Brooklyn Museum, where Shelley Bernstein is the Chief of Technology. Bernstein not only influences tech ideas at the museum she also helps them move the mission. They are doing some amazing things with the geo-location application Foursquare and it all started simply with the Brooklyn Museum experimenting with Foursquare. In a blog post, Shelley talked about the reason why they decided to explore Foursquare:

> As simply as I can put this, Foursquare is about place and identifying yourself through that. It is a celebration of the visitor—the people who crossed the river, who made it in the door and decided to identify themselves with us…right here at 40.67124,-73.963834.[6]

In one of their first experiments, members of the Brooklyn Museum staff took advantage of the neighborhood around the museum itself. They had other staff members, many of whom were local experts in the location, add tips about what was interesting for visitors to see in the neighborhood. As Shelley says in her blog, "as people explore our area, the Brooklyn Museum staff help them along in their journey pointing out the joys of pancakes at Tom's Restaurant or the killer wine selection at Abigail's." Soon people began to leave tips about the museum itself on its Foursquare page, which people then obviously get to see when they check into the Museum.

They also went a step above and beyond and used the gaming feature of Foursquare in their functionality. The person who "checks

---

[6]http://www.brooklynmuseum.org/community/blogosphere/bloggers/author/bernsteins/

Figure 4.1 Foursquare Mayor Offer
Source: www.brooklynmuseum.org/community/foursquare

in" to a location around the Museum the most becomes the "Mayor." In the Museum's version they awarded the "Mayor" with a free one-year membership.

That's a pretty good incentive! Not only does it encourage people to visit your location, it also encourages people to visit the location over and over again. The reward for being the mayor is one part financial reward, one part status symbol.

Innovation Driving Technology

Let's take a look at the opposite scenario: The process of innovation driving new technologies, which then change society as a whole. Examples of these can be seen in the process of creative destruction. The concept of creative destruction was first talked about by Joseph Schumpeter in his book, *Capitalism, Socialism, and Democracy* (first published in 1942). He says "The opening up of new markets and the organizational development from the craft shop and factory to such concerns as U.S. Steel illustrate the process of industrial mutation that incessantly revolutionizes the economic structure from within, incessantly destroying the old one, incessantly creating a new one ... [The process] must be seen in its role in the perennial gale of creative destruction; it cannot be understood on the hypothesis that there is a perennial lull."[7] This means that we are constantly moving forward in a creative process in a capitalistic market. The small main street stores of early times turned into the giant factories and monopolies of U.S. Steel in 1911 and Microsoft in 1995, which

---

[7]Joseph Schumpeter. *Capitalism, Socialism, Democracy.* (New York: Harper Perennial Modern Classics, 2008).

in turn, are overturned by the small Internet start-ups of today. This process repeats itself over and over. These are, of course, the same markets in which nonprofits compete with each other. Think of the impact that cancer-related nonprofits like Susan G. Komen, and now Livestrong, have had on large nonprofits like the American Cancer Society.

People like to think altruistically and pretend that nonprofits don't compete with each other. They do, though, and we all know it. Every dollar that comes out of your pocket to support a program is a dollar that's not necessarily going to another nonprofit. This is something that the nonprofit of the future needs to wake up and acknowledge.

We are not saying that, economically, this is a zero-sum game. There really is not a finite pool of money for nonprofits. There is almost always another dollar that another donor is willing to give. However each successive dollar needs to provide incremental value above and beyond the last dollar to convince that donor to part with it. Donor fatigue is the real adversary in the nonprofit world. Keeping your organization relevant to the needs of the donor and as visible as possible are two ways to keep your cause and organization top of mind. As donors integrate more technologies into their daily lives, there are more opportunities for your organization to interact with them. We'll talk more about this in Chapter 9.

Innovations Driving Technology in Africa: Solving for Water and Fires

You may think that it is a little random to present three examples of innovation driving technology in Africa here. However, the fact is that to really understand how innovative thinking drives technology, it is best to step away from high technology for a moment and get back to the basics. There are instances when a need drives the creation of a piece of technology that does not exist in order to fulfill the needs of consumers. These are some of the purest forms of needs driving technology and technology driving innovative solutions. The challenge exists in either creating the technological solution from scratch, or adapting existing pieces of technology to create a solution. Africa is a hotbed of technology innovation for the purposes of solving real world problems.

In Africa, water—specifically clean water—is a scarce resource and access to it is limited in some areas of the continent. The lack of access to clean water does not diminish the need for it. The acquisition and transportation of clean water is a real need for many communities, and yet there is an absence of technology to help solve this challenge.

Along with a lack of access to clean drinking water, many African villages have a lack of electricity. They are disconnected from the grid, unable to access even the most basic comfort of light in the evening, and this lack of access to electricity has created a life-threatening situation waiting to be solved by purpose-built technology.

Acquisition of Water. Worldchanging.org has written a number of articles about low-technology solutions that emerged from innovation efforts designed to answer and solve problems like these. One of the technologies that emerged was a kid-powered water pump that transformed the power from a merry-go-round into water.

> The children push the merry-go-round again and again. As they run, a device in the ground beneath them begins to turn. With every rotation of the merry-go-round, water is pumped out of a well, up through a pipe, and into a tank high above the playground.[8]

Just like Henry Ford leveraging existing pieces of technology from the meat packing industry in his automobile manufacturing process, the Roundabout Outdoor Company is using pumps and playground toys to deliver clean well water to villages in Africa.

Reinventing the Wheel. Access to clean water is only half of the challenge for some Africans. Transporting water, which weighs slightly more than eight pounds per gallon, can be an enormous challenge for villagers who can live miles away from a pump or water station.

> "At present water is mainly fetched by adult women in discarded plastic containers carried on their heads," notes Hendrikse.

---

[8]http://www.worldchanging.com/archives/000446.html

Figure 4.2   Photograph of Q Drum
Source: http://www.flickr.com/photos/emeryjl/3536992082/, http://creativecommons
.org/licenses/by/2.0/deed.en
Photo by James Emery, Creative Commons Licensed

> Bear in mind that in some cases these containers have an
> unstable weight, when filled, of 10 kilograms. The long-term
> result is invariably damage to the neck vertebrae.[9]

Hans and Pieter Hendrikse developed the Q Drum as a solution
to this transportation problem (see Figure 4.2). The need for a durable, low-cost water transportation system drove the invention of a new
piece of technology (or, more appropriately in this case, the reinvention of the wheel). Yes, the Hendrikse brothers reinvented the wheel
so that it was hollow, could be rolled on the ground and could hold
up to 50 liters (more than 13 gallons of water). The total weight of a
filled Q Drum could exceed 100 pounds. but because of its simple
design, it could be hauled by men, women, and even children.

Putting Out Fires. Beyond the need for water there is also a need for
light—safe light. It is commonplace for African villages to derive their
evening light from sources such as kerosene lamps. Kerosene lamps
not only emit noxious fumes when burning, but they are also a significant fire risk. Each year numerous villages experience fires due
to kerosene lamps being knocked over and catching fire. Beyond the
safety concerns, the cost of kerosene is so high that light has become a
near luxury item as "many households spend as much as 30 percent

---

[9]http://www.worldchanging.com/archives/000462.html

of their disposable income on fuel-based lighting—consumers receive little value in return. Fuel-based lighting is inefficient, provides limited and poor-quality light, and exposes users to significant health and fire hazards."[10]

The situation was so ripe for an innovation solution that the World Bank initiated a challenge program to generate solutions.[11] In 2007, the Lighting Africa Project began as an opportunity for private enterprise to drive alternatives to kerosene lamps. The project set out the opportunity as a challenge for innovators to develop an alternative technology.

Beyond Lighting Africa, numerous organizations and individuals have aimed to create technological solutions to this humanitarian challenge. Organizations such as the Solar Electric Lighting Fund (SELF) are using innovative applications of solar arrays to not only provide enough power to villages for lighting, but also enough power to support infrastructure, such as health care facilities in Rwanda, and laptops for education in South Africa.

The simplicity in the technology is not the important point of this section. The fact that there was a need and new adoptions of technology had to be created to fill the need is the point. There will be opportunities in your organizations to solve massively complex problems with the simplest of technologies. Innovation can drive creative uses and reuses of existing technologies. Each great idea has a multiplier effect: Clean water not only quenches thirst but it is a critical step in the elimination of water-borne disease such as cholera and provides irrigation for crops and livestock. Safe lighting and clean power are stepping stones that lead to health care and educational opportunities. Simple technologies can often have the most impact so long as their creation is purpose driven by innovation.

Interview: Webinars at NTEN

As we said, we really admire the Nonprofit Technology Education Network. We interviewed Brett Myer and Holly Ross from the

---

[10]http://www.lightingafrica.org/node/23
[11]http://web.worldbank.org/WBSITE/EXTERNAL/COUNTRIES/AFRICAEXT/ 0,,contentMDK:21461355~menuPK:258649~pagePK:2865106~piPK:2865128~ theSitePK:258644,00.html.

NTEN about their direct experience in driving technology innovation. They were kind enough to give us some insight into accomplishments within their organization. Looking back on some of their projects, even Brett and Holly are amazed at how rapidly technology gets adopted. It is inevitable that what is new today can be passé in just a few years.

David and Randy: Please give us an example of a time when your organization initiated and launched a truly innovative project. What was it?

Brett and Holly: Way back in 2004, we launched our Online Learning Series—our webinars. It doesn't seem innovative now, but we were among the first to do them.

David and Randy: How did the idea come about?

Brett and Holly: We were investing a huge portion of our then-tiny two-person staff into organizing six or so two-day technology conferences around the country. Organizationally, we had two needs to meet. First, we wanted to give members who couldn't come to our annual conference an opportunity to learn. Second, we only really had one other program, and we needed to become more than that annual conference. But, we were hitting the same four to six cities every year, and essentially ignoring the middle of the country. So while we were getting beyond the big annual conference, which we needed to do to sustain our organization, we weren't really meeting our mission very well. ReadyTalk was one of our exhibitors at our annual conference. With their help, we put together a proposal to the then-ED to try the new program with volunteer speakers.

David and Randy: What were the obstacles and opportunities discovered in the development process?

Brett and Holly:	It has allowed us to connect to a much wider audience. We get attendees from all over the world now. And the number of times per year that we can provide value to our community has exponentially increased. The format also allows us to pilot content. We can test out a topic and keep working on it at very low cost. So it's actually a tool that allows us to experiment. At first, we had lots of technical obstacles. It just wasn't a medium that anyone—attendees or presenters—was used to. We had a lot of public education work to do to get our community prepared to learn in this new way.
David and Randy:	What have you learned from the experience and how has that directly translated into a better organization?
Brett and Holly:	We learned that change takes time. That's a lesson we learn a lot at NTEN, actually. Getting people invested in webinars as a learning opportunity took a couple of years, but we made slow and steady progress until the market caught up to us. It's the same with a lot of our content. We have to hammer away at the same themes until people are ready to hear it. Sometimes they are ready because you've done such a great job laying the groundwork. Sometimes they're ready because some big topic hits the news and everybody's talking about it. You can't know it's going to happen for sure, but if you have the right idea, and you are slowly building momentum, be ready for when it does. Innovation isn't as fast as it's made out to be.
David and Randy:	Was there a formal process involved? If not, would it have been more helpful to have one?
Brett and Holly:	We didn't have a formal process, and I would have been waylaid if we did. I think the right

approach is to do a responsible amount of data gathering, and then propose something that mitigates risk while still allowing you to experiment and take the risks you'll need to take. The process we did, and still do, have in place that I think is critical is evaluation. It's vital that you evaluate the results and decide whether to scrap it, iterate, or go big!

■ ■ ■

This interview truly highlights some major points. The first point is that driving an innovative experience is difficult and that it takes time. As you begin to implement your innovation program at your organization, be equal parts diligent and patient. Dedicated efforts really do produce results in the end. And further, make sure that you are measuring the impact of your efforts. Benchmarking and evaluating your goals is important at all levels. Evaluation proves the value of your efforts, helps you stay focused, and can be used as leverage when you need additional resources to expand your efforts.

Conclusion

Technology and innovation go hand in hand. Technology is indeed driving innovation, and innovation is driving technology. IT is a dichotomy that seems to work. As technologists develop new technologies, brilliant marketers, communications professionals, community organizers, and the like find ways to leverage the new technologies for good. Simultaneously those same professionals are challenging IT teams in the market to keep up with their creative needs and develop applications and interfaces that will enable them to deliver on their missions.

The real insight in all of this is that innovation is coming at you from all angles. There is endless advancement and endless opportunities to drive advancements. Every nonprofit is equally capable of generating a breakthrough concept and finding the technology to fulfill it, and there is no reason that you cannot think of a novel way to implement a new technology you recently identified. What you are probably lacking is just the ability to actually do it.

If you do not have the capacity to innovate as part of your organizational culture currently (to move from idea to initiation or concept to action), then Part 2 of this book will help. In it, you will learn more about why your organization has been unable to turn great ideas into exceptional programs, and what you can do to change that. Part 2 is an in-depth look at the three core pillars that we believe form the framework of a successful and robust innovative organization. In order, they are: awareness, structure, and staffing.

THE THREE PILLARS OF INNOVATION

CHAPTER 5

Awareness

Where and how do you generate the new ideas and concepts to test?
This varies. You want to have many different sources or nodes
throughout an organization as well as external sources that can
feed into this. Ideas come from staff and volunteer leadership, from
monitoring trends, from individuals throughout management and
on the grassroots level who, through continuous improvement, think
of new and better ways of doing things and accomplishing goals.
      —Danny Ingram, Chief Mission Officer at the
                  American Cancer Society High Plains

Sadly, most nonprofits do not exert any energy or effort into awareness activities. When it comes down to it, being aware of your own business, your competition, and the environment is critical to the success of any organization. It should be a simple task. In most people's minds, building awareness is simply letting other people know about what you are doing. However, in this chapter, we are going to talk about information traveling in many directions. These include:

- Awareness campaigns that let people know who you are, what you are doing, and how people see you,
- Awareness campaigns that let you know what your competition is doing, and
- Campaigns to find out what the general market is up to.

79

In this way, awareness is a triple check on your efforts, not only in corporate communications but in every aspect of your organization. Employing the awareness techniques in this chapter will get you started in a continual pattern of self assessment, benchmarking against competitors, and seeking out insights from leading edge experts in all fields.

Knowing Your Own Business

The first step in awareness is becoming aware of your own awareness levels. Look closely at how your organization is promoting its efforts. What are the channels that you are using and, frankly, what are the results? As you self-assess your own awareness efforts, think of your core constituency and imagine how they use the channels you are using to build awareness. Now think about your future constituency—the new advocates and donors. Are you communicating to them?

When thinking about corporate communications, the first thing to understand is that the traditional awareness campaign is dead. The days of running a public service announcement (PSA) on your local radio or TV station or petitioning newspapers to create public awareness of your project or program are gone. The general public cares little about what radio, TV, and print media say. *Simply put, if you are reading this book we want you to reconsider everything your board or communications department suggests as an awareness campaign.* Every campaign that your nonprofit does should be built to drive a specific action, not just draw awareness to your organization or cause.

If you were properly aware, you would be thinking about advertising trends outside of the nonprofit arena. When a new company with a new product enters the space they don't have an awareness campaign to let you know that "Guitar Hero III" is here. They have an advertising campaign to let you know that you can now buy "Guitar Hero III" and you should let all your friends know so they can buy it too, play it collaboratively online, and have an outstanding entertainment experience. Few companies spend a million dollars on awareness campaigns; they spend millions of dollars selling the features and benefits of a product or service. However for some reason the modern nonprofit has in its head that advertising is bad and that it's not something to spend donor dollars on. This is utterly false.

Another thing to be aware of is the move of social entrepreneurship. A lot of modern social entrepreneurs such as Stacy Caldwell of Dallas, Texas, speak of the double bottom line in business. Social entrepreneurs like Stacy have two overriding principles that drive their businesses: Making a profit and making an impact. That could be in helping feed the under served or putting profits toward grants to nonprofits in their local communities. Think of Toms Shoes as an example of this idea: For every one pair of shoes they sell, they give one to a child in need. The mission statement about their One for One business from their website says it all:

> Using the purchasing power of individuals to benefit the greater good is what we're all about. The TOMS One for One business model transforms our customers into benefactors, which allows us to grow a truly sustainable business rather than depending on fundraising for support.[1]

Although a whole book could be written on the movement toward social entrepreneurship instead of nonprofits, think of this as something you must be aware of as a growing movement all over the world. Social entrepreneurs are pushing the envelope on cutting-edge marketing and communications techniques. Being aware of the developing field in its early stages could give your nonprofit organization insight into innovative techniques and methodologies to employ. They are the organizations that the modern nonprofit is, and will be, competing against, dollar for dollar.

Advertising Is Not a Bad Word

It's important to emphasize, then, that the modern nonprofit needs to see itself as a business that solves problems instead of selling widgets. Modern nonprofits should be spending money on advertising campaigns, not awareness campaigns. And if you do have an awareness campaign, make sure it has an action tied to it. The amount of information that is displayed to the average human being has never been higher, the signal-to-noise ratio has

---

[1]http://www.toms.com/movement-one-for-one

never been lower, and, frankly, an awareness campaign is not going to break through the clutter.

Being aware of this is absolutely critical to how you make the world aware of your organization. When someone wants to find out about your nonprofit they will Google it. Most of the time they will Google WHAT YOU DO not WHO YOU ARE. And if they do try and Google your name, they probably won't get the name right. We hear all too often how someone has searched for David's nonprofit "Lights. Camera. Help." but typed in "Lights. Camera. Action." or instead of searching by the right name, they remember it's a nonprofit film festival in Austin and Google that instead. No amount of awareness campaigning will change the small nuances of this behavior.

The modern nonprofit needs to begin running action campaigns. Action campaigns are highly directed advertising campaigns that have a point and call people to action. We look at advertising as an equation that, from the outset, balances the value of awareness and action. This formula is what we recommend you use to evaluate your current efforts and as a baseline for all your future efforts. Use this equation as you begin to form your messaging and then leverage your channels to both build awareness of your efforts and drive actual action. If you combine that with a model of paid advertisements on radio, TV, and online, asking for free in-kind donations or traditional PSA placements, then you have a true campaign that can compete in today's modern advertising market (especially at the local level).

The advertising has to be very clear, though. What exactly are you telling people? Every advertising/awareness action needs to have an equal or greater call to action. Think of it as an equation next time you review an advertisement for your nonprofit:

$$Adv = Awareness^2 + Call\ to\ Action^2$$

Once again think of who and what your advertising campaign is competing against. It's not your nonprofit versus the local Red Cross PSA that runs at two in the morning. It's your nonprofit against NIKE, Target, Walmart, Sears, Volvo, Ford, Chevy, and even that local guy that burns money while hocking furniture. And, to distort things even further, think of your nonprofit competing against the Humane Society's infomercials. As Raj Salwan writes in the Oakland Tribune about the recent ASPCA television campaign:

> The images are designed to inflame our anger and tug at our hearts. Severely matted dogs, wounded cats, and emaciated horses linger on the television screen and in our minds. Throughout the 90-second infomercial, celebrity voices plead with us to open our hearts, and our wallets, to save these poor creatures.[2]

Nonprofit leaders have evolved their techniques to include PSAs; we are talking infomercials that ask for donors to give $19.95 a month. How does your last advertising campaign stack up? Are your campaigns to develop awareness about your projects, programs, and organization as effective as your competitors'?

Modern nonprofits are using the same technologies that for-profit organizations are using to attract consumers. We are all using social media, search, and mobile communications to better target and market to constituents and reduce donor-to-volunteer acquisition costs. It's amazing to think about how two out of three of these major communication technologies were not even around five years ago! Now they reach 500 million to four billion people worldwide.[3]

Knowing the Surrounding Market

Environmental awareness can be defined as understanding the current state of things outside of your own organization. It entails how you view the external world and interpret what is going on in the greater environment. This awareness is often misunderstood as reading the right innovation magazine, or the most current management book.

Awareness is something that cannot be a burden carried by one individual. Awareness should be a small component of everyone's daily activity. Innovation opportunities appear on a daily basis and

---

[2]http://www.mercurynews.com/columns/ci_15152387
[3]http://www2.tbo.com/content/2009/mar/02/6-10-people-worldwide-have-cell-phones/news-money911/
  http://www.facebook.com/#!/press/info.php?statistics

the first step in becoming an innovative organization is becoming aware of those opportunities.

Conventional wisdom would say that to become aware of innovative ideas and concepts you should invest in scanning major aggregators of innovative ideas such as *Wired* magazine, or joining a trade group such as the Product Development and Management Association. These activities have their value, and they will always bring to your attention mature and developed ideas and concepts. However, the ideas that you will read and learn about were designed to solve problems and fulfill the needs of someone else's constituents— not yours. No one likes a copy-cat! So when you learn about other company's innovative solutions remember that they researched *their* customer needs and developed a solution to drive value to fit within *their* organization's future vision.

Awareness is at its most valuable when you have the ability to see technologies and concepts before they become widely adopted. Figure 5.1 shows a standard product lifecycle. The best time to identify

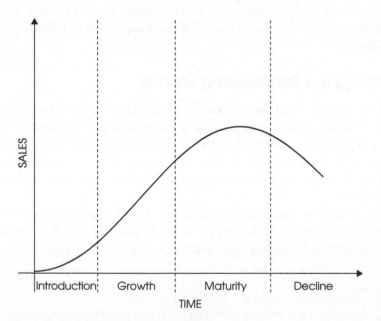

Figure 5.1   Standard Product Lifecycle
Source: Adapted from http://www.netmba.com/marketing/product/lifecycle/.

an innovation opportunity is during the introduction phase—also known as the early adopter stage.

There are many tactics to gathering and developing this insight and knowledge, but the underlying fact is that being good at awareness takes work and dedication. The more energy and effort you put into awareness, the more ideas you will find and the better you will be able to pinpoint competition in your marketplace.

Knowing the Competition

The search for competition is a scary thing to think about for most nonprofits but long gone are the days of nonprofits following a long and lonely road to accomplish their mission. The future of nonprofits is inherently tied to staying aware of competition and identifying other people to collaborate with it.

A simple example of this comes from the company HelpAttack!, which David co-founded. HelpAttack! is a fun and easy way for you to turn social actions into social good. It lets people pledge an amount of money for each action you take in the social web, and then gives it to your favorite nonprofits. Their idea of awareness is simple and one we can all learn from. It is based on the fundamental idea that we all need to simply keep our eyes and ears open. This is something that is ingrained in the mindset of all HelpAttack! employees and board members.

When a HelpAttack! employee or board member comes across anything remotely similar to their product out in the marketplace, they are asked to let the organization know. This has resulted in almost a hundred emails to the Chief Executive Officer and Chief Operating Officer about competing products, and those emails are then researched and archived for future comparison in their project management website called Base Camp. This idea of sharing awareness is a competitive advantage within their culture and something all nonprofits could bake into their new employees and volunteers.

Knowing how to conduct an effective awareness effort into your competition is also half of the battle. The following pages feature some of the best sources for new and breakthrough ideas in the nonprofit space. Everyone has their own preferences and what we have listed here are just a few suggestions to get you thinking about the sources available to you. It is meant to serve as a roadmap but by no means is it a comprehensive listing.

Subscribe. Subscribing to periodicals is a great idea and it will yield a substantial volume of information. The challenge has always been what to subscribe to. Some magazines like *Wired, Fast Company, The Chronicle of Philanthropy, Philanthropy Today,* and *GOOD* produce a lot of current and innovative business ideas. However, the ideas they write about tend to be mature, implemented concepts, and, in most cases, are being featured because they are already successful. Matt Glazer, Partner at GNI Strategies, told us this in an interview: "I make it a point to read 100 pages of articles a day and bounce ideas off my coworkers. Nothing sparks innovation or creativity more than talking through what smart people have already figured out."

We suggest that if you are seeking to be on the leading edge of innovation you subscribe to blogs, podcasts, and Twitter feeds from the top minds in development and theory. These are the sources of the technology that is driving the advancement in social media. Understanding the direction that the actual technology is headed is like tuning into the weather forecast. It gives you a sense of what is coming before it actually begins to impact your day.

The following people are innovators in the field.

Marc Canter, Broadband Mechanics Marc Canter is CEO of Broadband Mechanics, which produces People Aggregator, a social networking tool with source available. He was a founder of the company that became Macromedia, and blogs on Marc's Voice, frequently critiquing other Internet luminaries and competitors. Canter is also a contributor to many open standards efforts and advocates for end-user–controlled digital identities and content (being a co-signer of the Social Web Users' Bill of Rights) and has written on the multimedia industry, micro-content publishing, and social networking.

Dr. danah boyd, www.danah.org Dr. danah boyd earned her master's degree in sociable media at the MIT Media Lab, after which she began studying teen behavior and identity online. She documented what she was observing via her blog (www.zephoria.org/thoughts/), and leveraged her research and insights into a successful career. Danah earned her Ph.D. with a designated emphasis in new media from U.C. Berkeley School of Information. Her dissertation was entitled "Taken Out of Context: American Teen Sociality in Networked Publics," and focused on the use of large social networking sites such as Facebook and MySpace by U.S. teenagers.

Beth Kanter, www.bethkanter.org   Beth Kanter is a trainer, coach, and consultant to nonprofits in the area of effective technology use. She has worked on projects that include training, curriculum development, research, and evaluation around the use of new media tools such as blogging, tagging, wikis, photo sharing, video blogging, screencasting, social networking sites, and virtual worlds to support nonprofit goals. In 2009, she was named by *Fast Company* magazine as one of the most influential women in technology and one of *BusinessWeek's* "Voices of Innovation for Social Media." In March, 2009, she served as the 2009 Scholar in Residence for Social Media and Nonprofits for the Packard Foundation.

Howard Rheingold, www.rheingold.com   Howard Rheingold was a founding executive editor of *HotWired*, one of the first commercial content websites published in 1994 by *Wired* magazine. After leaving *HotWired*, he founded Electric Minds in 1996 to chronicle and promote the growth of community online. In 2002, Rheingold published *Smart Mobs*, exploring the potential for technology to augment collective intelligence. Shortly thereafter, in conjunction with the Institute for the Future, Rheingold launched an effort to develop a broad-based literacy of cooperation. As of 2008, Rheingold was teaching courses at U.C. Berkeley and Stanford University.

Chris Brogan, New Marketing Labs   Chris Brogan is President of New Marketing Labs. He works to improve online business communications through the use of social software, community platforms, and other emerging web and mobile technologies. Chris Brogan is a 10-year veteran of using social media and both web and mobile technologies to build digital relationships for businesses, organizations, and individuals. Chris speaks, blogs, writes articles, and publishes media of all kinds at www.chrisbrogan.com, a blog in the top 10 of the *AdvertisingAge* Power150, and in the top 100 on Technorati.

Bruce Sterling, Wired.com   Bruce Sterling is an Austin, Texas-based science fiction writer and Net critic, internationally recognized as a cyberspace theorist. As well as being a leading science fiction writer, Bruce Sterling has been involved with numerous projects and written several books of futurist theory. He was the founder of the Dead Media Project, an on-line reliquary, or archive, to forgotten or dead media technologies. In this way, he looked to the past through the future, anticipating, almost, in the shininess of new media, its utter destruction. He frequently identifies and wryly rails against future trends at the SXSW interactive festival. www.egs .edu/faculty/bruce-sterling/biography/.

Joe Ito, Creative Commons   Joe Ito is CEO of Creative Commons (www.creativecommons.org). He is a co-founder and board member of Digital Garage JSD:4819 (www.garage.co.jp) and is on the board of CCC TYO:4756 (www.ccc.co.jp/eng/) and Tucows AMEX:TCX (www .tucows.com/). He is a Senior Visiting Researcher of Keio Research Institute at Shonan Fujisawa Campus in Japan. He is the Chairman of Six Apart Japan (www.sixapart.jp/), the weblog software company. He is on the board of a number of nonprofit organizations including The Mozilla Foundation, WITNESS (www.witness.org/), and Global Voices (www.globalvoicesonline.org/). He has created numerous Internet companies including PSINet Japan, Digital Garage, and Infoseek Japan and was an early stage investor in Twitter, Six Apart, Technorati, Flickr, SocialText, Dopplr, Last.fm, Rupture, Kongregate, and other Internet companies. He maintains a weblog (joi.ito.com/) where he regularly shares his thoughts with the online community.

Holly Ross, Nonprofit Technology Network (NTEN)   Holly Ross has spent more than five years at the NTEN, listening to the NTEN community and developing webinars, conferences, and research that will help members use technology to make the world a better place. Holly is the editor of *Managing Technology to Meet Your Mission: A Strategic Guide for Nonprofit Leaders*, and came to nonprofit technology after working for social change at CALPIRG. www.netsquared.org/blog/holly-ross.

Brian Solis   Brian Solis is author of a new book on social media and business called *Engage!* He is Principal of FutureWorks, an award-winning New Media marketing and branding agency in the Silicon

Valley. Solis is globally recognized as one of the most prominent thought leaders and published authors in new media. A digital analyst, sociologist, and futurist, Solis has influenced the effects of emerging media on the convergence of marketing, communications, and publishing. We especially love his coverage of PR 2.0. www .briansolis.com/about/

The Staff at Mashable.com   The staff at Mashable who report on nonprofits include some of our favorites such as Frank Barry and Geof Livingston. Within the digital advertising, marketing, and social media screen, Mashable.com presents a continuous stream of insightful opinions on the latest trends and technology development. Unlike gadget sites like Engaget and Gizmodo and technology sites like CNET, Mashable presents stories with a focus on cultural impact. Mashable is a valuable awareness tool because it allows you to see how people are using technology and the impact it is having on their lives.

■■■

Most of these personalities have been active in this space for years and, although the web is young and social media is younger, there is an expansive amount of new ideas from just these few writers. There is additional value in learning from who these personalities find valuable, too. Pay attention to the people they refer to in their writing, as well. By taking this approach (starting here and branching out), you can create a reading list of blogs and Twitter feeds to skim every morning, and podcasts to listen to on your commute.

Participate. Beyond listening and reading it is crucial to become an active part of the conversation. Leaving comments on blogs, and even initiating your own and attracting comments, is an active way to tease out ideas and thoughts with the best minds, for free. The critical part of participating is investing the time and the effort to honestly be an active and acknowledged member of a community. After enough genuine comment conversation and forum/social media discussions, you will have access to dozens of collaborators who will not only help you out in developing your own organic ideas but will point you to new, up-and-coming technologies. This is how you become an *early adopter*. For instance, we, as authors of this book, would love to be a part of your network and refer you to people as you enter the space. Please connect to us on our website at www.thefutureofnonprofits.com.

Learn. Every day there are thousands of web-based seminars going on at little to no cost. The investment is in the time it takes to focus on the topic and engage the presenter. Combine the collaborative value of social media, and being in a modern nonprofit engenders sharing and cooperative effort. This directly translates to an abundance of free content filled with useful and powerful ideas.

Make a point to register for seminars early and often. Dedicate at least an hour each week to attending one that is of particular value to you. And remember to take it seriously. Turn off your email, your cell phone, and Tweetdeck and hold all calls. To get the most awareness value out of these webinars, you have to be fully engaged in them, not a passive participant.

A few examples include:

- www.nonprofitwebinars.com

  Nonprofit Webinars provides educational and professional-development offerings for trustees and staffs of nonprofit organizations. They offer a wide variety of presentations on an increasing number of topics.
- www.nten.org/events/webinar

  NTEN delivers professional webinars and content designed to teach nonprofit organizations to skillfully and confidently use technology to meet community needs and fulfill their missions.
- www.ted.com/talks

  TED Talks is a series of video recordings of presentations from the TED conferences. They deliver inspiration all with the central theme that each TED presentation is an idea worth sharing.
- www.poptech.org/popcasts

  PopCasts are video presentations from PopTech, a unique innovation network—a global community of cutting-edge leaders, thinkers, and doers from many different disciplines, who come together to explore the social impact of new technologies, the forces of change shaping our future, and new approaches to solving the world's most significant challenges.

Confer. Get out of the office and on the road. Attending the right conference could mean hundreds of thousands of dollars to your organization. In the futuring and innovation arena there are as many conferences as there are days in the year, and selecting the right conference can be a daunting challenge. It is important to pay very close attention to the topics and the credentials of all of the speakers. Look at how they intend to present their topics and the angle they are taking. In some cases you can see the same presenter multiple times at different events and their perspective is unique and fresh each time to better accommodate the audience.

In terms of awareness and innovation, remember that the conference participants are as valuable as the presenters themselves. In some cases the participants can add more value to your organization than the presenters can. Use your time between sessions and during meals to meet people and explore the collaborative working opportunities. Often participants are there to connect with each other and leverage those contacts in the development and distribution of their own projects. You may even find the next big thing over a casual cup of coffee between break-out sessions.

Here is a list of some select conferences and why we think you should consider attending.

South By Southwest (SXSW) Aside from the fact that we enjoy this festival because we have presented at it nine times between us, it is also a hotbed for innovative ideas and thinking. SXSW draws in nationally known speakers for a four-day interactive festival every spring. This conference routinely features digital media business ideas and concepts that permeate the general public 12 to 18 months after the conference. This is an event where the interactions with the participants are as valuable as the presentations from the speakers. Everyone has a startup they are working on, everyone has a new concept, and everyone wants to share it with you. Conferences like SXSW not only inspire but they can generate awareness and opportunity if you put the effort in. The number of nonprofit-focused panels is growing every year and continues to impress. And in 2010 SXSW even started to offer scholarships for nonprofits to attend.[4]

NTEN'S NTC Conference   The Nonprofit Technology Education Network's NTC conference is an annual nationwide conference on technology and nonprofits. The event draws participants with a variety of backgrounds from an array of agencies. Everyone from Convio to Microsoft to Blackbaud and Google attend this event. It is ideal to attend and learn from the best and brightest in the nonprofit field. And of course thanks to the folks at Convio they have a great scholarship program as well (www.nten .org/scholarship).

NetSquared   NetSquared is a set of smaller regional conferences produced by a technology consulting group called Compumentor. We have found NetSquared to be a high-value event where smaller nonprofit organizations come together and present case studies of their work in social media. It is a great event to attend to learn about the possibilities of social media and see what is currently being done. Attend this event for inspiration and to view what is possible when your organization is aware, structured, and staffed properly for social media innovation.

BarCamps   Find local BarCamps. These are usually free, one-day collaborative events with discussions, demonstrations, and interaction from participants who are the main actors of the event. David is a co-founder of a nonprofit BarCamp in Austin, Texas, and a co-founder of VideoCamp Texas. For example, VideoCamp Texas is a free one-day ad-hoc gathering of video, public relations, new media, and marketing professionals, born from the desire for people to learn about the best practices in online video production and distribution in an open environment. You can learn more at www.videocamptexas.com. We really enjoy the nature of camps and the free flow of information and transformations that can come out of them for people at all levels of expertise.

---

[4]http://501derful.org/info-tech/sxsw-wants-more-nonprofits-and-they-are-paying/

Explore. Right now there are dozens of organizations online seeking to reward innovative ideas. You can benefit from their work if you know where to look. Idea incubators, web-based concept evaluation competitions, and angel investors are continuously seeking the next breakthrough business concept. You should be sifting through this content for highly valuable insights to apply to your organization. We like sites such as:

- Quirky.com: (www.quirky.com)

  Quirky is a site that allows those with ideas to engage a community of product influencers. Quirky seeks to identify the best new products and crowdsource improvements. The best part is that those who submit their constructive criticism receive compensation for providing constructive feedback.

- Idea Crossing's Innovation Challenge: www.innovationchallenge.com

  The Innovation Challenge is the world's most established business innovation competition. Since 2003 the brightest and most creative graduate students have been matched with leading companies such as Harley-Davidson, Hilton, and IBM in an experience designed to address our most pressing business and social innovation challenges.

- FutureThink: www.getfuturethink.com

  Futurethink is an innovation consultancy that helps organizations enhance their innovation capabilities by arming them with the tools and techniques to translate theory into practice. Futurethink offers the largest catalog of innovation research and tools in the world, along with the most comprehensive innovation training curriculum anywhere, with more than 250 resources and tools, and more than 40 courses focused on critical innovation topics and techniques.

Crowdsourcing. There are also companies that can help you tap into the collective intelligence of thousands of people all at once. The concept is called crowdsourcing and, essentially, it is asking a crowd for simultaneous feedback, evaluating it, and then using the best data from the effort by applying it in your business. Most of the organizations are crowd-funded by individual donations and crowd-sourcing is a way to bring in ideas from your stakeholders.

In particular, Idea Rally (www.idearally.com) is a great way to conduct student-based crowdsourcing. It leverages the collective intelligence of a select set of participants in order to identify a broad range of solutions. And for the fundraisers reading this, check out Kickstarter (www.kickstarter.com/start), where people attempt to crowd-fund their projects from films to album releases.

Get Local. In most major cities there are local Social Media Clubs and 501 Tech Clubs. There are developers, marketers, futurists, and social media mavens who live in your city that want to share their experiences and ideas with you. They have ideas about new programs that can benefit your organization, and they are looking for an organization to help them pilot them. If nothing else, the conversations at these local events are stimulating and topical. Search scheduling sites such as Meetup.com, Upcoming.com, and even Twitter for local meetings and go!

The Value of Awareness

Awareness is the key to understanding the current and future state of your industry's environment, the Internet landscape, and the social proclivities that will drive the trends of the future. Awareness combined with a future view delivers a plan to create and launch meaningful campaigns, Internet-based activities, and develop timely innovations.

Investing time, effort, and funds into awareness is absolutely critical to your success now and in the future. It is a daunting challenge and not one that should be taken on by any one person. Much as we discussed in the HelpAttack! example earlier in the chapter, awareness has to be a collaborative staff and volunteer effort for key reasons.

Having a specific job function such as chief awareness officer may sound effective, but if you do that you will only get ideas and concepts filtered through one point of view. Every organization that centralizes awareness into one person runs the risk of creating a biased information-gathering process based on the perspective of one person.

Remember every employee and volunteer has a unique view into your organization and sees different opportunities. The more minds you have exploring valuable innovation applications, the more solutions you will find. For every challenge there is someone who wants to find a solution, so encourage them to do so. Build this type of awareness into every staff and volunteer you have in your nonprofit. Awareness is one of those situations where the more opinions you have, the better.

Example: American Cancer Society

Innovative social media ideas and platforms are out there just waiting to be leveraged if you are aware of them. In 2004, the American Cancer Society (ACS) attended an Association of Professional Futurists Conference (www.profuturists.com). While there, they saw a newly launched technology called Second Life (www.SecondLife.com). Second Life was an online community technology that used a video game-esque interface so that your digital self (your avatar) was able to move about a communal geography and interact with other community members.

The ACS considered the technology and its fundamental purpose of helping people organize a community online in a digitally immersed environment. Just being aware of the technology was insufficient, though. They had to understand its potential. ACS set out to engage the community and develop a presence, and to do it they used the same community development techniques that have worked in communities all over the country for decades.

Because they were aware of Second Life in the early adopter stage, ACS became a predominant philanthropic backer in Second Life and parlayed their initial 2005 awareness and fundraising experiment into four years of increasing participation and income development. That $300 conference ticket led to the development of a program that has attracted more than 4,000 volunteers and $878,000 through the 2010 season.[5]

This brings to light the value and importance of awareness within communities and forces us to ask questions like, "What do you do once you find something of value? How do you turn an idea

---

[5]http://wiki.secondlife.com/wiki/Relay_For_Life_of_Second_Life

or a concept into something that generates income or moves an organization's mission forward?" We strongly believe an important factor in leveraging an idea into a product exists in getting support and direction from your organization's leadership.

The Importance of Leadership

Leadership drives culture. In a recent *New York Times* article, Stephen Sadove, chairman and chief executive of Saks, said this about culture and how it relates to the financial bottom line:

> Culture drives innovation and whatever else you are trying to accomplish within a company—innovation, execution, whatever it's going to be. And that then drives results. When I talk to Wall Street, people really want to know your results, what are your strategies, what are the issues, what it is that you're doing to drive your business. Never do you get people asking about the culture, about leadership, about the people in the organization. Yet it's the reverse, because it's the people, the leadership, and the ideas that are ultimately driving the numbers and the results.[6]

If Steven Sadove were to weigh in on where awareness begins he would probably say that it begins with the organization's leadership. Executive leadership sets the expectation of a culture of awareness and establishes it as the responsibility of every employee and volunteer. The culture of participation, inclusion, and collective responsibility are what derive real value from awareness activities. It's essentially more eyes looking for more ideas and trying to solve more problems.

Of course, inevitably, part of awareness is getting things wrong, too. There will be trends that you identify that do not come to fruition, and there will be technologies that you see promise in that fail. You will see and miss opportunities because you cannot move fast enough, or they are based on fleeting fads that never take off. The key is that, in doing awareness exercises, you make a full

---

[6]http://www.businessweek.com/innovate/content/jun2010/id20100610_525759.htm

faith effort, especially in today's competitive business environment. In terms of failure, noted blogger and entrepreneur Jason Cohen writes, "A lovely new company/customer etiquette has emerged, and small (internet) startups are especially suited for exploiting it. I hope you're not ignoring it. Here it is in short: 'People readily forgive honest human error, but become adversarial and distrustful with the typical, sterile customer/provider relationship.' Your donors, board members, and constituents will forgive you if you fail so long as you are approaching innovation earnestly. In the terms of Cohen's statement, your leadership must hold your innovation program to the following standards:

- You do your honest, level best to do right by your customers, evidenced continuously through all your communication (tech support and/or website) and not just after a crisis.
- You learn from your mistakes, evidenced by problems tending toward the esoteric, and explain what steps you've taken to avoid failure and similar classes of error.
- You do everything in your power to be the best, evidenced by a culture of awesome employees and inventing new ways to make your customers successful, so mistakes are ordinary human error, not negligence or indifference.

Cohen, like your stakeholders, wants, "to work with other people who behave like real people, who are obviously trying their best, and who respond to problems as earnestly and quickly as can be expected."

In our opinion this is really a common scenario for most non-profits. Your executive leadership is so scared of making a mistake that it's created a culture that demands perfection at all times. Although it's often repeated and mocked in our culture, mistakes need to be made for great innovations to emerge. Nonprofits that are scared to make mistakes will *never innovate*. We don't think we can emphasize this point enough. Low- and mid-level nonprofit employees must be allowed to try new things. They must be allowed to innovate and fail. Stop being so perfect!

Interview: Social Media Innovations with Robert Quigley

Leadership must have a major hand in promoting a culture of innovation. This is a very important step toward successfully innovating.

Unfortunately, most small businesses and nonprofits are not set up this way. This is particularly true in the world of old media newspaper publishing.

The following interview with Robert Quigley, Social Media Editor for the *Austin American-Statesman* newspaper, is a great case study regarding the benefits of having a leadership team that identifies and supports innovation. We sat down to interview Robert to find out his ideas on bringing old media into the future of journalism through the new technology of social media...

David and Randy: How and what innovations did you start at your current or past job?

Robert: I started the *Statesman*'s Twitter and Facebook efforts. In the summer of 2008, I started tweeting as the @statesman, becoming one of the first news organizations in the world that actually conversed personally with the public using social media.

David and Randy: How did the innovation effort get initiated?

Robert: I was using Twitter personally for several months before I started using the @statesman account. I thought it was a fun service, and I noticed that people were often sharing news (in the form of links), including *Statesman* news. It occurred to me one night while I was up late that I could tweet news as the *Statesman* itself, and ran to my computer to see if anyone else was doing it. I found a blog that tracked newspaper Twitter accounts, and to my surprise, most major newspapers had a Twitter presence. I noticed that all but one were using RSS feeds to post news on Twitter, and that those accounts all had very small numbers of followers. The *Chicago Tribune*, using @ColonelTribune was the one exception— the *Trib* was posting news in a conversational tone using the colonel persona, and it not only had more followers than the other accounts, it was engaged with the audience. Having used Twitter for several months, I knew that people didn't want to use the service as an RSS reader, and the *Tribune* had it right. I went into my boss's office the next morning and asked whether I could start posting as the @statesman. Within an hour, I had sent out our first tweet.

David and Randy:	Do you have executive support for your efforts?
Robert:	I have always had incredible support from the executives for not only this venture but everything else I've tried. My supervisors are social media users, and they see the value in engaging the community. When I was named Social Media Editor in the summer of 2009, I was one of the first to hold that title in the news industry. Without that type of support, this would not have worked.
David and Randy:	How is your role/department structured? Does your leadership/management give you more freedom to experiment with new ideas and concepts?
Robert:	I report to the Managing Editor for the Internet, Zach Ryall, who reports to Editor Fred Zipp. I am given quite a bit of freedom to try new things. In fact, a large part of my job description is to stay abreast of the latest social media trends and to find ways to use them at the *Statesman*. When I have a new idea or tool I want to use, I bounce it off Zach, explaining the benefits and costs (in terms of money or manpower), and we work together to figure out the best way to implement (or, rarely, turn down) whatever it is I'm bringing to him. I'm given a lot of leeway to try new things. Thanks to that, not only have we pushed ahead with Twitter more aggressively than most, we were also a very early adopter when we teamed up with Gowalla, we gave Google Wave a try when it was hot, we experimented with lifestreaming using Posterous, live video, live chats, and much more.

What Leaders Should Tell Their Teams

So, as a leader with an active stake in innovation in your nonprofit, what should you pass on to your employees and future managers? We really like these simple, five keys of innovation that Wayne Bundy, Ph.D., shares in his book *The Art of Discovery*. They are:

1. Be deeply immersed in your profession.
2. Carry out diverse research projects and maintain worldwide exchange.
3. Have a profound hope of causing a ripple in the wisdom of the world.
4. Free your mind of thought constraints.
5. And find the strength to defy the conventional.

We have obviously given numerous examples relating to the first key of innovation Bundy presents. It's about being active, participating, and conferring within your business and its community. For example, neither of us has ever been in a finance role at a nonprofit, but we have taken nonprofit accounting classes and could read and explain nonprofit accounting statements. This is very much a part of "being immersed in our professions."

Robert Quigley's story about the *Austin American-Statesman* speaks to the second key innovation factor and just how critical to business running diverse research projects is. The *Statesman* could have said no to Quigley when he approached them about starting to use social media but instead they let him research and experiment. Now the *Austin American-Statesman* has more than 27,000 people getting their news daily from Twitter.

Regarding the third key, although it's an ephemeral concept, it's also why most of us work in nonprofits. We are not content to sell widgets, or computers, or cameras. We want to change the world.

The fourth key is another ephemeral concept but it's easy to make the real-world leap. For David, his best ideas around problem solving and innovation come during running. It's on these pre-planned exercise trips around neighborhoods he is familiar with that his body switches into automaton mode and his mind is free to think about the problems of the day, the week, the month, and beyond. He created the SharingHope.TV idea during such a run. Another great example of this comes from Sarah Vela. Vela is the CEO of HelpAttack! (where David serves as chief operating officer). Vela came up with an idea while sitting at a traffic light in Austin, Texas. She had recently come out of working on fundraising for the Movember campaign and figured there had to be an easier way to give. Her mind cleared as she waited at that long stop light and the idea formed.

Vela's idea also lends itself to the fifth key. It would have been easy for Vela to sit at the traffic light, think of the idea, and say, "that's a cool idea," and then keep driving and never act on it. Instead she wrote it down and started to think more and more about it while talking to more people about it again and again. Not less than a month after her idea originated, she had a management team lined up and after that came incorporation as a technology start-up in Austin.

One of the challenges in innovation is identifying innovative leaders who are not scared to make mistakes and take risk in order to generate cultural shifts. It is this kind of leadership that is required to guide an organization into the future. But where can we find these leaders?

Jason Cohen writes on his blog:

> Not one of the successful entrepreneurs I know *started* as an expert. Rather, career and expertise are developed simultaneously, eventually resulting in success when coupled with a few key events. . . . Sergey and Larry weren't advertising experts before they started Google. Joel Spolsky wasn't a blogging expert before starting FogCreek . . . In fact, in all these cases, it would have been impossible to have been an expert! Why? Because Google reinvented advertising, there were no 'blogs' when Joel started posting essays . . .[7]

The great leader your organization needs is not necessarily someone who has years of experience driving innovation and start-up businesses. What he or she needs to have is a willingness to be aware of the situation you are in, the eagerness to explore emerging opportunities, and the tolerance when those opportunities

---

[7]http://blog.asmartbear.com/expert-distraction.html

do not turn into huge successes. Become aware of the internal resources that you have, and you may be surprised by what you find (and we'll talk more about this in Chapter 6).

Conclusion

Awareness is just the first step in the innovation process. It is good to be thinking both inside and outside of the organization, and considering the larger forces that are acting on your nonprofit and the causes that you are engaged in. Without awareness you are devoid of the inspiration that you are going to need to drive innovation into your nonprofit. But what happens once you actually bring the inspiration into the office?

Having big ideas is not enough. Having executive leadership that backs the concept of innovation is also not enough. You have to have a plan on how to develop and leverage those ideas and, more importantly, you need an organizational structure that supports that development. Without a structure that will empower people and nurture ideas, all of the brilliant ideas that awareness generates will go to waste.

In Chapter 6, we look at the successful and unsuccessful ways that organizations structure themselves. We give you insight into how we have organized solid innovation structures within companies and offer you strategies to implement yourself in nonprofits of any shape and size.

CHAPTER 6

Structure

INTO THE BELLY OF THE BEAST

When a resolute young fellow steps up to the great bully, the world, and takes him boldly by the beard, he is often surprised to find out that it comes off in his hand, and that it was only tied on to scare away the timid.

—Ralph Waldo Emerson

Once you have an awareness program in order, you will soon see yourself in possession of an abundance of great ideas. The real value is not only in the ideas but in the projects and programs that they evolve into. It is through this development process that you will decide what ideas have the most value to your constituents and your organization.

Structure Provides Value

Having a well-organized and managed development structure is absolutely critical to ensure that the right ideas are getting the right amount of funding and attention. A great structure not only acts as a quality control mechanism but it also shields rapid prototypes and innovations from outside forces. Your structure is as much about nurturing and protecting the new innovations from the outside world as it is protecting the outside world from your innovation. If you invest resources, time, and energy into building awareness, make the next step and prepare your organization structurally to make the most of what you find.

If we believe that innovation is 99 percent perspiration and 1 percent inspiration, then structure is at the heart of the perspiration. Structure is what is going to allow you and your organization to take concepts and turn them into reality. Structure is what regiments the development process just enough so that it can be efficient and flexible.

Developing a structure that can deliver on both efficiency and flexibility is a key component to any productive innovation program. In the Innovation and Commercialization 2010 McKinsey Global Survey, one of the biggest challenges expressed by participants was the need for better innovation organization. In fact 42 percent of survey respondents said that improvement in innovation organization would make a profound positive impact on their ability to drive innovation. Interestingly enough "organization" was closely followed by "developing a culture and climate that fosters innovation" as the second biggest challenge. Ding! We already covered driving that culture from the top down in Chapter 5.

The study goes on to point out that executives consistently credit and blame the same two things for their successes and failures in innovation development: The relationship between research and development (R&D) and marketing, and the process for translating an idea into a functioning prototype. Whether they succeed or fail, the process for translating an idea into a prototype is one of the top two determining factors. We think that having a defined and properly functioning process to make that translation inherently creates a positive working relationship between R&D and marketing over time and projects.

The McKinsey report says it best:

> Organizational factors, including innovation-specific processes and links to support functions, remain a challenge. As hard as it is for companies to implement organizational changes in increasingly complex environments, the results suggest that when companies make the effort, they will experience more success with innovation.[1]

---

[1]http://www.scribd.com/doc/38658368/McKinsey-Global-Survey-Innovation-and-Commercialization-2010

It is time for you to take a serious look at how your organization is driving innovation development. Without a refined and flexible structure that works well with your organization, your innovation development process will never be as efficient or effective as it could be.

Hindsight Is Always 20/20

In order to build the future, generations of scholars have told us to look back before looking forward. However, this way of thinking is fraught with errors. How do we recognize the truth from our own histories? How do we avoid the rose-colored glasses of the past? Robert Penn Warren said, "History cannot give us a program for the future, but it can give us a fuller understanding of ourselves, and of our common humanity, so that we can better face the future."[2]

First, ask yourself this question: "How can I change my structure?" It's a great question and there is no easy answer. Structural changes begin with:

- Understanding where you are currently,
- Identifying an optimal state, and then
- Making adjustments to process in order to make that optimal state a reality.

Structural change is one of the most difficult things to accomplish. In a large organization, change is difficult because there are a number of stakeholders involved. In small organizations, change is difficult because everyone is constantly collaborating in an ad hoc ballet of organized chaos. The dreaded reorg threat that is bandied about at many nonprofits is a perfect example of this. However, for a lot of organizations, reorganizing is much needed and much overdue.

Follow the Idea

The best way to understand your structure is to follow an idea. It need not be a great idea, or even a good idea. The point is that you want to learn where new ideas go to be recognized, vetted, developed, and sometimes die. How do you get your idea into the struc-

---

[2]http://hnn.us/articles/1328.html

ture? Is there a "good idea" drop box that you place a response card into by the lunch room? You know, the moldy and cobwebbed one in the hallway. Or maybe it is an e-mail address "Suggestions@ yourcompanyname.com." Potentially there is a department that accepts requests for all things 'new product,' but in most cases you are going to go to someone you know, or the administrator of the department that most closely aligns with your product idea. Is it income generation, patient/constituent service, advocacy, government relations, finance, or corporate communications?

Once you find the decision maker, do you have the opportunity to advocate for your idea to them? Is there a time set aside to help them understand the value and impact this idea could have? Can you reach the decision maker and converse with him or her about your concept and actively answer questions about your innovation? Do you get the chance to listen in on the conversation beyond the two of you: The questions and concerns about who is going to fund this, who is going to run this, and who is going to get the credit for this? Or are you pretty much shut out of the process once your idea enters the suggestion box?

What happens next—after you relay the idea—is absolutely critical to understand! Your idea will be looked over, considered, possibly pondered. At that point, the person reviewing the proposal may realize that they lack the human and financial resources within their department to implement the innovation. You may hear "no," or a polite "maybe." You may even hear the dreaded, "let's look at this again in six months," and "let's put this into a committee" but the reality is, your idea has died.

Your idea died for two reasons, and they are both related to structure.

Death by Lack of People

The first death your idea died was death by lack of people. The department head that reviewed your idea may have loved it, but he or she completely lacked the human resources to turn it into something, foster it, and watch it reach its full potential. As we will discuss in Chapter 7, his/her staff are very, very busy at working. They are doing their jobs and have no time to remove themselves from the task at hand.

Have you heard this before? We talked about similar thoughts in Chapter 5, where there was no time to look up from the present work to pay attention to the evolving environment around you both inside and outside of the organization. Now, in the ideal scenario, we lack the time to try and develop a new project or program prototype within a group. The department head is not getting rewarded or acknowledged for the innovative product idea that you just handed to him/her. His/her role and responsibility is to drive the core metrics prescribed by the organization's structure, and taking staff from their current roles to try out your prototype idea is not one of them.

Death by Lack of Budget

Your idea died a second time because of the way that nonprofit budgets are created and function. For the most part, in the organizations we have worked for, and with, in the past, there is no funding for projects and programs outside of the budget forecast made 12 months prior, often three months before the fiscal year started. There is no room to develop new programs and ideas as they arise because there is no budget to support anything you did not have in mind and well-defined when budgets were submitted.

Worse still is the fact that no department head will ask for a chunk of money for a project that is not well-defined, delivers no known return on investment (ROI), and frankly has not even been thought of yet. No one will take that risk, and no budget director will tie up that money when it can be allocated to a proven program that can use the funds for expansion. The worst case scenario is that your idea emerges just after budgets are submitted, and you have to wait 12 months for the next budget cycle (and 15 months before you can begin spending money). The best-case scenario is that you just get your idea in and approved and only have to wait three or four months to start development. Neither situation is acceptable in today's rapidly changing environment.

Hit the "Like" Button

We understand this exact scenario of the death of an idea, and know you do too. We have all felt the same frustration. Before launching a certain project we were told on separate occasions that there was no budget, no man power, and a staff member was blocking the project because they just had this feeling it was not a good idea. We were told to, "wait until they retire and try to push it through then." How ridiculous is that? Is that how you want to deal with innovative, game-changing ideas at your nonprofit? Yet, think for a moment …how often does this exact situation happen at your current organization?

There is almost nothing more frustrating than identifying a surging trend or an upcoming technology and being paralyzed and unable to act on it. In our experience of innovating in the social and digital media space, fundamental to implementing new social media technology is having an organization and people that are prepared to take the necessary steps toward experimenting, trialing, and rolling out an innovative program.

Key Elements of a Structure Ready to Innovate

Within structure there are key elements we need to draw attention to, and actively work toward integrating to help your organization prepare to leverage and adopt new innovative social media tactics and programs.

1. Experimentation: Organizations must be open to experimentation and have well-defined channels for new ideas to enter an evaluation process.
2. Encouragement: Organizations must encourage and support their staff in investigating new uses of technology, as this is what a lot of innovations take the form of.
3. Evaluation: Organizations have to have a consistent and systematic way of evaluating the potential value of the ideas they collect.
4. Reward: Organizations need to reward initiative and creative thinking.

Let's take a look at each of these attributes and see how you can craft an organizational structure primed for innovating.

Experimentation: Enabling an Entrepreneurial Spirit

Our world is fast-moving and continuously changing. It is teeming with aware and entrepreneurial minds consistently driving new products and applications to market daily. Project development time and product lifecycle have to be compressed many times over thanks, in large part, to digital technology. To be effective and leverage new concepts your organization needs to have a sense of experimentation and act, in a sense, like a startup company. Learn from the structure and processes of startups and try your best to replicate their light and fast innovation development methodologies. Think of some recent social media start-up companies that spent a significant time in Beta testing like LinkedIn. (Even Gmail, Google's mail service was in Beta for five years from 2004 to 2009.) These startups used limited trials to prove concepts and identify viable strategies while limiting budget and effort investments. They moved quickly and took every advantage of being light and nimble.

The traditional program management approach that nonprofits take is too slow and costly. There are specific obstacles that structure must address if the entrepreneurial spirit is to thrive in your organization. As you design your structure think lean, fast, and unobstructed. Startups can move from idea to prototype faster than you because they do not have the bureaucratic obstacles to jump through to secure permissions, funding, and resource allocations. Some of these obstacles include project management offices, integration processes, and exhaustive executive approvals. Time is of the essence so developing and maintaining a structure that permits and even helps rapid proof of concept work divert around substantial time intensive processes is critical to success.

Don't think "outside the box," think "off the beaten path." Advocate for an approval process that does not require initial approvals, where everything that comes in gets an initial green light and then approvals are sought after the concept has been fully vetted by a select cross-departmental team. Consider establishing a very small fund or budget line item to evaluate and prototype new ideas. The most effective way to quickly drive value is to create an insulated development channel free and clear of traditional oversight and roadblocks.

This idea may seem scary; a fund without multiple layers of oversight? A process not governed and regulated by three committees? A place devoid of posturing, power grabbing, and project ownership fights? It sounds like Utopia to us! What is scary is falling behind your competitors and failing to capitalize on great ideas and inspiration from your own internal entrepreneurs.

An example of social media moving faster than the pace of project development is a podcasting series attempted by a health nonprofit. This example highlights the need for a specific structure and set of rules for innovative project development.

The organization thought that it would be a good idea to initiate a podcast series on cancer. They had good awareness around podcasting as it was a new technology at the time and just coming onto the radar screen. They were perfectly positioned to have been early adopters and were going to put human and financial resources behind an innovative project that would position them ahead in the market. They were going to be innovators in the field! However, the development team did not have a structure or a process that allowed them to move quickly enough to keep pace with the ever-advancing environment.

In this instance, it took the core team nearly a year to review the technology options, evaluate the alternatives, make a decision on an implementation direction, and initiate a purchase order for the requisite technology and hardware to begin the podcasting program. By the time they released the first podcasts they had spent nearly 20 months on the project. By the date of release, podcasting was into the early majority phase of the product lifecycle. They were no longer early adopters and innovators—they were part of the "everyone else" crowd. Furthermore, at release, there were free online podcasting solutions available, rendering their technology purchases 18 months prior unnecessary. The podcasts themselves were well produced and professionally edited, but not well received, and the development model they used clearly illustrated the inability of a rigid structure to keep pace with innovation, especially innovation in the digital realm.

Encouragement: Offering a Place for Ideas

Encouraging your staff and volunteer networks to submit innovation ideas is critical to staying current in an evolving landscape. We already covered this in Chapter 5 in terms of awareness. (One of the most important constituencies to engage is the newly hired staff, and we'll talk more about this in Chapter 7.) How you bring in and process their ideas and the recognition that they receive will have a lasting impact on the future success of your innovation program.

In 2002 the American Cancer Society set out to create a formal structure that would capture, evaluate, and quickly develop social media concepts and other breakthrough fundraising and patient-service innovations. The program was called Springboard and it succeeded because it was designed to leverage the intelligence of the entire organization and sought to engage them all in the identification of the best and most valuable ideas.

Springboard became a well-known collection channel that the Society promoted to its staff and its volunteers. The Society published articles about Springboard in their newsletters, created internal memos for the staff, and promoted it through various departments in order to engage as many employees and volunteers as possible. With each additional person engaged, Springboard became that much more valuable; more eyes looking for more opportunities. As a direct result of the continuous outreach, Springboard brought in hundreds of ideas for formal consideration each year.

Evaluation: Looking for Winning Ideas and Implementing Them

As an innovation program, Springboard was a success because it created a formalized structure to collect ideas, evaluate their value, then develop them independently of the traditional organization's bureaucracy and reward the staff and volunteers who submitted the concept. The inherent value in the structure of Springboard is that it significantly decreased the time and cost of developing a new program while significantly increasing the volume of new projects and programs being offered. In addition, it drove interest in new product development into the organization as a whole.

Once an idea was received, the Springboard process directed the idea to a select group of employees with very diverse job functions for review. By attaining multiple points of view on an idea, the Springboard process ensured that each innovation idea was thoroughly vetted. The team changed from year to year but, without fail, marketing, finance, mission, operations, and corporate communications were represented. The American Cancer Society intelligently involved staff from all corners of the organization; divisional, national, and even local employees. This intentional diversity created a Springboard team with deep experiences and a wide perspective on how an idea could impact every level of the organization. This is an intentional structural choice that everyone can learn from.

From our interview with Lisa Goddard, Capitol Area Food Bank

Q: How is your role/department structured? Does it give you more freedom to experiment with new ideas and concepts?

A: Online marketing is part of the Mobilizing Communities team which consists of Advocacy and Public Policy, Resource Development, Community Events, and Marketing and Branding. As Online Marketing Director, I supervise one person who is responsible for the organization's online development and fundraising goals. My direct manager is responsible for all marketing, communications, and branding.

I do have freedom to experiment with new ideas and concepts. Many of those ideas come through the scheduled brainstorming meetings I lead, through digital communication trainings I conduct internally, and by participating in cross-departmental meetings. I also use a variety of project management tools to document processes and stay organized. All of these combined create a fertile ground for creativity and inspiration.

Springboard had its own budget independent of any department which gave the team the ability to fund idea development without approvals and without extended conversations about departmental ownership and oversight. The structure was simple—the Springboard team went through a number of reviews and made a determination if the project would drive mission and have a strong ROI. The evaluation steps that they went through and the criteria that they used were keys to their success.

Since Springboard was an incubator for new ideas from 2003 to 2008, the majority of those ideas leveraged the power of social media. Because they were evaluating numerous social media ideas simultaneously, it was important for the team to understand the business drivers that were behind each submission. If you remember, in the introduction we talked about the need to understand the pain points of our constituents and then surprise them with meaningful engagements. Those same kinds of initial questions were asked at ACS when evaluating the value of a new idea.

A secondary function of a good innovation development structure is to test the feasibility of a program or idea and if it can be implemented to scale. Because the Springboard team was structured the way it was, the team could evaluate the scalability and feasibility of an idea before they ever spent a dime or an hour on prototyping. If the team saw a solid business case and a potentially implementable idea, they would allocate funding to prototype the idea. By using a protracted development timeline and a limited budget, Springboard identified, evaluated, prototyped, and commercialized products in a fraction of the time and at a fraction of the cost of traditional product development, and this is the point of innovation: To develop new and relevant things, quickly and efficiently.

The next part of the innovation process, then, in this sense, is that it allows you to thoroughly screen ideas for potential value, and then rapidly turn those ideas into prototype programs. The key word in that statement is thoroughly. Cursory reviews of ideas by one person do not constitute a thorough examination. You have to look at ideas deeply to see where their true value lies. Sometimes an individual idea's value does not truly emerge until it is paired with an existing program or another concept. Engaging a diverse innovation review team as described above will help ensure that you are seeing an idea for all of its potential value.

Think of the innovation development process like a ship moving through the Panama Canal. Along the route it will need to pass though gates, and at each gate it needs to be inspected and allowed to move along or be turned back. The same is true for this development process, outlined next. We encourage you to use this as a base model and amend it to fit your organization's needs.

Step One: Discovery. Gather submitted business concept descriptions. Be proactive and solicit ideas from your staff and volunteer network. Create challenges for them by posing particular questions and asking for solutions, and have an open channel for people to send in their unique ideas for consideration. Look through all of the ideas you receive and see if there are any patterns in the ideas being suggested.

Make sure that you pay particular attention to staff or volunteers that send in uniquely interesting ideas. A great sample of technology enabling this to happen is the City of Austin's website SpeakUpAustin.org, which is centered around voting for new city projects and runs forums powered by uservoice.com.[3]

Step Two: Scoping. Give concepts an initial review against your criteria. Here are just a few of the criteria we have found that help us identify the most valuable and viable possibilities: Scalability, Sustainability, Cost Basis, Defined ROI (income or exposure), Tie to Organizational Mission, and Capacity for Execution. This is where your process begins to pay off. By weeding out unsustainable ideas early on you preserve development energy and funding for viable ideas. The questions that you ask in this step are critical to the success of your program, so invest a lot of time considering these questions with your review team. Have your review team evaluate the idea and if the concept satisfies the criteria, move it on to the next stage of evaluation.

Step Three: Develop a Business Case. Once approved, engage the person who submitted the idea to draft a business plan of their concept. The business plans should thoroughly outline the mission, goals, evaluation tools/metrics, and resources for the prototype. We believe a completed business plan is a formal application for funding. At this point we suggest your review team (consisting of at least five to 10 people from all different areas of the organization) closely review these business plans. The business case will be a useful document in the near future. If the prototype is a success, you can use the business case as a showpiece for executives and as a roadmap when the project moves from prototype to permanent program. If the team approves the business plan, it passes through gate three.

Step Four: Conduct Constituent Market Research. Engage the idea submitter to commission a market research study to determine what demand exists for their concept. Ideally you already know the problem it is going to solve and the value it will bring your constituents. Now you need to see if there is a market for it. Your research can be as

---

[3]http://austin.uservoice.com/forums/61425-city-of-austin-taxi-service

complex as engaging a firm, or as simple as creating an online survey to poll friends and current donors. If demand can be quantified, fund the prototype concept as per the business plan and pass gate four.

Step Five: Development and Testing. Create a rapid prototype to prove the concept works. In an ideal situation we suggest that you aim to prove the concept within a nine- to twelve-month time frame. Remember the purpose is to prove a concept, not create a new program. We strongly encourage limiting funding to below $20,000 if you are a large organization or $5,000 if you are a small one to encourage bootstrapping and keep the effort focused. When the prototype period is over, review the outcome and decide to pass gate five, or cut the program and create a learning lesson from the exercise.

Step Six: Launch. If chosen for implementation, work closely with the idea submitter to identify the resources and department support best suited to deliver the program to market, and arrange the smooth transition and success of the new program.

■■■

As you can see from this process, the structure is not just in place to help guide an idea along, but it is also a risk-mitigation device. By constantly checking the proposal for feasibility, demand, and ROI you are making sure that your new product-development efforts have a better chance of yielding winners. Nothing is ever certain, but this kind of a process helps deliver well-vetted concepts quickly and affordably.

Reward: Acknowledging Idea Contributors

Finally, the most critical piece of an innovation program process is rewarding those who submit ideas for consideration. You need to find a way to publicly acknowledge contributors. It reinforces the value of the program, the commitment of the organization to innovation, and draws additional interest and submissions. Staff and volunteers who have the opportunity to develop their products fully should receive substantial recognition from your national leadership and their peers. In many cases their new products will contribute to the organization for years to come and you should make a point to recognize their hard work.

In some more successful organizations we have seen innovation prototypes lead to promotions, awards, and outside speaking opportunities. Depending on the scope of the innovation program, the idea submitters have helped create a new department exclusively to produce and market the program. Within the social media field, there are many innovation projects which have gained recognition at conferences and in media, and the program developer is usually who is given the credit and opportunity to present them. For instance, as we mentioned briefly, we have been fortunate enough to present our digital media innovations at the annual South By Southwest (SXSW) conference a number of times.

Another Way to Support Ideas

To this point we have talked about innovation development within the boundaries of the formal structure of your organization. But what about innovation that occurs outside of your walls? How do you handle organic innovations that you do not control? We understand the concerns and need for a sense of control over the messaging, branding, and the other corporate communication specifics associated with outreach. Our recommendation is straightforward: *Support volunteer innovation activity outside of your formal structure.*

The ability to support and manage volunteer activity outside of your formal structure is a key component to your future success. Today's volunteer is not content to work 40 hours in your office doing menial labor like licking envelopes or folding napkins for your gala; they want to work short periods of time and have a dynamic and visible impact on your nonprofit. Before you even begin to recruit the new generation of volunteers you need to have a structure in place that can accommodate their desires to give back to the organization in ways you have never thought of.

Social Media Breakout

If your volunteers are well-versed in the digital world, they will want to leverage their own social media savvy for the good of your organization. Remember that concepts like social media websites and forums are being developed, launched, and executed outside of your organization. In the past most of us would have backed away and put distance between ourselves and these "unauthorized activities."

The reality is, though, that these activities and events are occurring more frequently and you should create a mechanism to embrace and manage them when they come to your attention. From a structural perspective we see two ways that you can approach these quick, innovative social media innovations.

Launch and Learn!

Your volunteers are using online initiatives to drive public relations (PR) campaigns and peer awareness. From a management perspective, strive to embrace blogger and author Beth Kanter's idea of "Listen, Learn, Adapt" or as we like to say "Launch and Learn!"

In the rest of this chapter, we look at two structural approaches for engaging digital volunteers who are using social media for social good. One approach is passively watching volunteers leverage social media to promote an organization, and the second is an organization that fully embraces and engages their volunteers and the power of social media.

From our interview with Weston Norton, Filmmaker

Q: Most valuable thing you have learned both tactically and strategically?

A: Decide and go. Don't wait till you feel like you know everything you need to know about something before you can take action or you may never do anything. It is easy for me to get bogged down researching and refining an idea without ever acting on it. That's partly because I enjoy that kind of work, but it's easy to use it as an excuse to not put something out there, especially working in media where successes and failures can be so public. However, particularly with online media, people are usually a lot more forgiving than you expect. It's more important to be consistently putting work out there—blogs, videos, newsletters, live streams, and so on—than it is for everything that goes out the door to be perfect. There is an old joke I used to hear on film sets when I worked in production: What did the brain surgeon say to the other brain surgeon? Relax, we're not making a movie. Of course you want to do the best you can, but relax and have fun with it.

Social media for social good is a relatively new term and one that we helped coin, and it is undeniable that social media is starting to revolutionize public relations for nonprofits. One of the concepts behind social media for social good is volunteers using their digital networks to support your good causes. There are two ways you can structurally align and prepare your organization to leverage this energy: passively and actively. Next we offer up two case studies: one, dealing with passive engagement, and the other, in active engagement.

Passive Engagement. The first annual Austin, Texas Tweetup (using Twitter to gather friends for a meeting) Blood Drive (ATBD)[4] is an ideal example of the impact an organized and connected group of volunteers can have when they leverage the power of their social networks independently of an organization, even when that organization does not directly engage their efforts.

A group of socially conscious volunteers made a concerted decision to use their social networks and social media outlets to attract blood donors to the ATBD. The volunteers wanted to push the idea to the contacts in their networks and see the impact they could have. They reached out through Facebook groups, Twitter, email, blogs, and Flickr, and were able to contact local traditional media such as KUT Austin, the *Austin American-Statesmen.*

The results are telling; well over 100 people attended the ATBD on the Thursday before a major holiday weekend. The example speaks volumes about the power that individuals have to mobilize a community with current free tools. All in all, two dedicated and motivated volunteers drove an event with no help from the nonprofit itself.

Structurally speaking, the local blood bank that organized the drive was not prepared to engage the volunteers and help them make the most of their passion and talent. What they did do was provide the volunteers with the critical information that they needed to spread the word and drum up support for the event. They were structurally prepared to address external volunteer engagements like this, even if they were only able to offer minimal

---

[4]http://www.youtube.com/watch?v=7DdkLMGtQnM

support. They did not say no, they did not claim copyright, and they did not actively work to shut down the volunteers' efforts. They allowed them to launch a PR campaign outside of the organization's traditional channel and reaped the benefits.

Too many times we hear anecdotal stories or read articles in the paper of how a nonprofit organization spent time, effort, and money closing down a paralleled fundraiser or PR campaign because it was not running through "the official channels." That is a clear sign that your organization lacks the structure to create fast and mutually beneficial partnerships. Your volunteers are identifying needs that you are not: Serving the community and driving solutions toward enacting the service—this is the heart of innovation. The best thing you can do is have a structure that welcomes their ideas.

Active Engagement. In this example, an organization directly engages their volunteers and helps them make as much impact as possible. In 2009, a group of friends in the United Kingdom decided to do a tweetup to support one of their favorite charities, Charity: Water. Charity: Water is a nonprofit organization bringing clean, safe drinking water to people in developing nations. They give 100 percent of the money raised to direct project costs, funding sustainable clean water solutions in areas of greatest need. Just $20 can give one person in a developing nation clean water for 20 years. Charity: Water became aware of the effort and directly engaged the volunteers, helping them spread, expand, and execute their concept.

In fact, the Austin, Texas Twestival (a festival organized through Twitter) was part of a worldwide event that took place in more than 200 cities on February 12, 2009. The Austin event raised $8,868.[5] Globally, the Twestival raised more than $250K for Charity: Water, providing the funds needed to bring access to clean water to more than 17,000 people. It is enough funding for 55 water projects in three countries. The key to their global success was Charity: Water being *aware* of the developing opportunity and having a *structure* to support it.

■ ■ ■

---

[5]http://www.youtube.com/watch?v=mKqJwNfLOmk

With these two examples in mind, think about your own organization and how it might react to a group of volunteers bringing ideas to their attention and wanting to execute similar programs. Think about who the volunteers would ask, and if that person would know what to do, or if they would pass the volunteer on. Structure extends all the way down to the front line staff. They have to know what to do when opportunities present themselves, and should be rewarded when they capitalize on them.

Meeting Volunteers in Their Networks

Including social networks as part of your structure is now the new normal. If you are still driving your traffic to a main website, please stop. People live, breathe, and donate on social networks. In the current and future online world, it is and will be absolutely critical to reach your volunteers and donors where they are.

The sheer size of social networks is stunning. In an April 2010 Mashable post, Muhamed Saleem compared the U.S. population to the Facebook population with stunning impact. When 116 million people of the 309 million people comprising the U.S. population are on Facebook, there is a compelling argument to get active in that community.[6] Every nonprofit should have a presence that is constantly updated on all social networks that you can afford to be on.

As important as maintaining a quality website is being an active participant in multiple online networks. Beyond the main social networks, be keen on the most topical networks that pertain to your industry no matter how small they seem. Be brave enough to start your own social network like the March of Dimes did at www .shareyourstory.org. The March of Dimes has seen a respectable growth on its social network in terms of users, but what they have found is that the active users are more involved and passionate about the cause.

Harnessing the Power of a Dedicated Community

The March of Dimes made an investment in its own organizational structure by creating the white label social network "Share Your Story." Share Your Story provided them with a structural advantage

---

[6]http://mashable.com/2010/04/05/facebook-us-infographic/

over other organizations by creating a hub for their volunteers to share and trade ideas about how to help the organization. The March of Dimes used the social network to gather information from their constituents, generating a greater awareness of their specific needs and wants from the organization. The network space also gives constituents a direct line into the organization so that when they need support executing a novel idea, March of Dimes is able to quickly assist them. When the March of Dimes needs to mobilize social action they can depend on the kinetic energy that resides in the ShareYourStory.org participants. Social networks in all forms, shapes, and sizes will become the destination sites and core communication channels replacing websites and e-mails. Be prepared for this shift and your organization will prosper.

A good example of this shift done properly comes from General Motors. In their awareness activities, GM identified an opportunity to communicate directly with its core customer base online through the social network arena. They initiated a social media engagement effort by hiring a social media manager at GM, Adam Denison. Adam writes in the PRSA *Tactics* issue 567 that you should, "build a relationship with the group administrator(s). The phrase group administrator sounds kind of technical, but really, they're very similar to editors in a publication." He goes on to say, "…when I join a group on behalf of GM the first thing I do is introduce myself to the group administrator and let them know I'm an available resource to them. This has worked very well and usually makes the group administrator feel pretty important because they now have access to an inside source."

What Adam found was that he was able, as an industry insider, to deliver credible and important information to numerous people who were eager to hear it. In his situation, he had the ability to reach out to the constituents running the largest Corvette group on Facebook and give them inside exclusive information about the 2010 model. In an instant, Adam made the group owners feel like *Road and Track* journalists. He even goes a step further, asking the bloggers and Facebook administrators to come to the same press events that the newspaper and magazine journalists do. This is great constituent relationship management practice, and proof that social networks are going to further become critical pieces of volunteer management in the near future.

General Motors provided Adam the opportunity to experiment in the online space and drive results. In addition they provided Adam a structure for success. The innovation is bringing the most loyal consumers into the inner circle previously reserved for an exclusive for journalists. GM was able to identify this opportunity and created a structural component to engage the opportunity.

It's Okay to Just Listen, Too. Even if you don't have inside information to share with all of your constituents, sometimes people just like to know the organization is listening. Being proactive and actively participating in related groups on Facebook, Twitter, Flickr, and MySpace further builds connections with your constituents year round. Sometimes you will have a story to share, sometimes just a link to new research, and sometimes you want to take the opportunity to just listen. If you do not have a structure that allows this kind of engagement, you are missing out on all of these opportunities to communicate with constituents. It's all about joining the conversation and being an active participant and contributor. Your audience is already talking about your story online and spreading your message, it's time you join in.

In Beth Kanter's and Alison Fine's book, *The Networked Nonprofit: Connecting with Social Media to Drive Change*, Fine talks about the three types of nonprofit organizations:

- Fortress: high walls; us versus them
- Transactional: what do you need from us?
- Transparent: talk to us, we talk to you, here is what we are doing

Their descriptions relate most closely to how the organizations interact with their constituents, but there are underlying structural components that support the various models. We understand that there is an overriding sense of us versus them that is pervasive in this field so we advocate for organizations to move as close to the transparent model as possible. Changing your structure to promote transparency can help you attract new volunteers and their new ideas, and that can lead to new innovations.

In a transparent organization both the successes and the failures are held up for examination and scrutiny. In fact, in organizations that are structured to learn from their mistakes we have seen better innovation development because innovation development teams avoid *repeating* mistakes.

Structurally speaking, a transparent organization will welcome and draw people to interact and contribute. Going back full circle to the question we posed in the beginning of this chapter, we want you to ask yourself, "How does an idea generated from a volunteer or donor move through my organization? Does my group or organizational structure support its development?"

Conclusion

This chapter offers examples of business events happening all over the Web right now. Volunteers at organizations are leveraging social media to their advantage and creating a structure external to your organization so that they can support your cause. We hope that you see there is a marked opportunity to gain volunteers and raise funds in both listening to staff and volunteers inside your organization, and supporting their outside communications.

The challenge is to be aware of those staff and volunteers trying to help and engage. Ask yourself if your organization is structurally prepared to support their efforts. Once you get your awareness program bringing in ideas, and your structure is prepared to handle and process the ideas effectively, it is time to see if you have the right staff in the right roles to maximize the innovative ideas that you are developing.

As we said at the outset of this book, our innovation program has three pillars. None is more important than the others but they deliver exponential value when implemented in order concurrently. The last part of this equation is staffing and it is the most difficult component to address. You are probably not properly staffed to innovate and thrive in today's digital world. You either lack the correct resources, or you have them but they are misaligned.

Chapter 7 offers insight into how to identify, develop, and retain the right staff and get them engaged in the innovations so their contributions will make the most impact.

CHAPTER 7

Staffing

THE RIGHT PEOPLE, THE RIGHT SKILLS, AND THE RIGHT ROLES

I think, at a child's birth, if a mother could ask a fairy godmother
to endow it with the most useful gift, that it would be curiosity.
—Eleanor Roosevelt

Chapters 5 and 6 discussed important strategies within two of our core components of successful innovation—awareness and structure—with emphasis in social media, where the environment is filled with innovative individuals and companies constantly churning out new concepts and products. There is a third core component that is also a crucial resource for everything we're discussing in Part 2 of this book, and it will determine the type of success your organization has. It is the people.

Hiring with an Eye toward Innovation

Historically nonprofit organizations have done an exceptional job of hiring staff, especially at the higher levels, to perform the various jobs required to move their mission. It is not surprising at all that a number of the staff we work and consult with say that when they find a nonprofit with a mission that fits them, it is a first-choice destination for them and other career-oriented individuals. With

125

billions of dollars in revenue, the nonprofit industry is a competitive space in the quest for good talent.

So while you are hiring the right people to move your mission, you should also take a step back and ask yourself if you are hiring the right people to drive a culture of innovation. It is as much a philosophical question as it is a question of function. The physical or intellectual ability to perform the tasks involved in innovation do not necessarily predict an individual's ability to drive value into your innovation program.

Beyond capability and capacity there is an intrinsic intangible that exists in each of us that drives us to be curious, and to experiment and explore for answers. That inherent curiosity is what you should be looking for in your candidates.

Although staffing is the third component of our innovation program, it has a direct impact on the effectiveness of the first two components as well. The staff and volunteers that you task to engage in the various steps of innovation have a lasting impact on the final products as well as the way your development process works. Innovations are like pieces of art in the sense that the personality and creativity of those crafting them are embedded in the final product. Selecting the right people to handle and oversee innovation development is critical, and, to get a great pool of people to choose from, your human resources department needs to learn to prioritize, prize, and hire for curiosity.

Although you may think if you are heavily engaging in awareness exercises, it automatically activates curiosity in an organization, you should further ask if you have the right people engaged. In Chapter 5, we talked about getting a good base of people engaged in awareness to ensure that there is a wide variety of ideas coming in for evaluation. With that in mind, have you reached out to the sometimes digitally savvy and knowledgeable millennial staff and challenged them to move the organization's mission forward through social media awareness?

Have you created awareness challenges around public policy, fundraising, and corporate communications, and directed those challenges to specific high-achieving groups? Are you sending your young and eager staff to local meetings where their ideas will be challenged? Where will they be exposed to new concepts and have their minds opened? Have you opened up Internet access to allow your entire staff to explore the web for inspiration? Or have you restricted your network prohibiting access to Facebook, Second Life, BoingBoing, Mashable, Tumbler, and Twitter? In addition, are you sending department directors to conferences with program coordinators so that they can explain all of the technology and how it will impact the industry? Or are you sending all of the executives to conferences that focus on high-level strategies without talking about tactical technologies?

Staffing Solutions

In order to critically look at your staffing situation, start by asking yourself a few key questions. First, consider if you have the right talent in your organization to effectively launch an innovation program. Then, think about where those key talented employees are within your organization. Finally, ask yourself if you know how to attract the best possible talent for the situation if you find out that you are missing talent. Let's look at these questions one by one.

The Right People
1. **Do you have the right staff and volunteer talent to move an innovation program forward effectively?**

The skill set you include in your current job postings is not going to cut it. We know. We checked. Trust us. You are still looking for a traditional nonprofit employee who has the skill set and passion to get the work done. What you need to be looking for is the candidate that can go beyond the job you are posting for and make contributions outside of the role. If you are relying on your existing job descriptions to find the right person, you are not going to find them.

If you are hiring for communications, you are looking for someone who has a digital presence and knows how to manage it. Someone who can be found on Google, and whose Facebook page is information dense and well maintained. You want someone who not only knows about blogging, but actually blogs *and* Tweets. Please see Appendix 1 for the basic description for a social media/ community manager intern that we created. This application will help you better understand what skills and traits you are looking for as you move forward in your search for web savvy social media interns to ramp up to full-time social media employees. It can also be easily adapted to fit part-time and full-time communications people.

The Right Roles
2. **Do you have them placed in the best possible location within the organization's structure so that they can make the most impact?**

Once you have acquired the talented people you need to make innovation a core part of your organization, you need to know how to manage them. You hired them, in part, to experiment and explore social media and identify new and interesting technologies that will help your organization grow and prosper. You also hired them to manage fundraising programs, be an administrative assistant, and coordinate volunteers. Do not lose sight of the value they bring outside of their job function, and do your best to help them find the balance between their explicit job duties and the extra contributions they are excited to make. Also make sure they have a clear career path in the organization. What does your career ladder look like? Does it really lead up? If so who was the last person to climb from the bottom to the top? Or do people climb up then switch ladders and organizations? That is a problem, as well. Remember to hire for ambition. No one wants to stay a Manager of Interactive Media for the next five years. And if they do, then you hired the wrong person.

In our experience, smaller organizations have a much easier time empowering and managing their staff than larger corporate organizations. The reason is that in smaller boot strap nonprofits every staff member is working multiple jobs simultaneously, so they hire flexible people who can multitask out of necessity. Smaller organizations rely on their staff to do more, while larger organizations tend to encourage their employees to adhere to their job functions because there is other staff to handle the rest of a process. Larger, more corporate organizations tend to have rigid structures and formalized job functions that discourage the kind of staffing we are advocating. Just because larger organizations tend to be more rigid, though, does not mean they do not have the capacity to be innovative. Once they get a system in place they can be very effective innovators.

Placement does not always just mean the department a staff member works in or the job that they take. In many cases the manager that they work for can have a great impact on their development in a job. In the past, we have each worked for managers who challenged us to extend our thinking on projects beyond the conventional. Pairing talented and curious new staff members with supportive and insightful managers can create a foundation for culture innovation to flourish.

The Right Skills
3. How do you identify the best talent?

Not only does the modern nonprofit need to do their research, they also have whole new arenas from which they can find and recruit candidates online. From Campus2Careers.com, to Careerbuilder, to Craigslist there are numerous options for finding not just new talent, but the right talent. If the online job site wants to charge you to post, contact them and apply for a nonprofit account.

We strongly suggest you do a quick environmental scan to see if your town has local nonprofit groups such as Nonprofit Technology Network (NTEN), Social Media Club, 501 Tech Club, Association of Professional Fundraisers, or The Young Nonprofit Professionals Network (YNPN). Clubs and networks such as these tend to attract the kinds of forward-thinking individuals that you want working for you. Make sure that you check with as many organizations as you can about recruiting from their members since all of them will usually post your job listing for free. Feel free to send us job descriptions to post to the community at www.thefutureofnonprofits.com.

In turn, go to their meetings and listen to their presentations since it won't cost you anything and you will come away with knowledge you didn't have before. Getting face time with some of these groups can generate long-term relationships and open doors to volunteer opportunities and engagements. For instance, while at the American Cancer Society, we engaged with a group of very talented volunteers in Second Life. By attending community meetings and special interest groups we were able to attract and retain the brightest and most talented volunteers and use their skills in computer programming, architecture, and event planning to initiate a truly innovative fundraising program that to date has contributed more than $800,000 in income and is still going strong. Knowing where to be was half of the challenge in finding staff and volunteers.

Also think of your work networks, and don't just rely on human resources to make connections. If your fundraising department has its own email newsletter that goes out to staff and volunteers, it is a good place to start seeking candidates. Ask them to include the posting on the back page of all of your official communications with donors and volunteers. And do not stop there! Do the same for any internal communications your organization puts out. You never know who may have a friend or a former colleague that may fit the position you are looking to fill.

Managing the Talented People You Hire

If you hire well, think about retaining them. In many cases, staff members will be more interested in their ancillary innovation development work than their primary job functions. Be creative and tie in both sides of the job. Part of retaining employees is identifying what is rewarding to them about the different components of their jobs, and feeding them additional responsibilities based on what they enjoy. This goes back to incorporating innovation as a success metric measured during yearly performance reviews.

If you have frontline staff that you know have the propensity to be outstanding contributors, find a way to encourage and measure their ability to bring in new concepts from the volunteers and community members they interact with. Set a goal that they will identify three unmet needs each quarter. In addition, tell them they will have to get solutions from the volunteers and community members that they interact with. This provides your income development staff or field staff another opportunity to connect. It also challenges them to find meaningful ways to improve the overall performance of the organization.

The experience of engaging constituents beyond their job responsibilities helps them learn about the potential good that your organization can deliver and builds a stronger bond. Empowering them to take the next step and create a proposal to act on identifying solutions tells them that they are trusted and valued members of the whole organization. By putting energy and resources behind their ideas, and giving them the chance to develop a program that drives the solution, you are giving them valuable experience. This, in turn, makes them more valuable to your organization.

The truth is, in an ideal world the innovative staff and digital savants would work long enough to really understand your organization and begin the opportunity to research, pilot, and eventually manage their own programs to drive the organization's mission forward for years to come. Not all organizations have that kind of patience, flexibility, or funding, though. However, with this in mind, how do you think you can empower your innovators and provide them a career path within your organization? Disenfranchised staff members are like poison to a nonprofit. If they feel there is no long-term place for them, they find any opportunity to mentally check out. You don't want them becoming internal slacktvists, do you?

Recognizing the contributions of innovators becomes even more critical in tougher economic times, since management styles change with the economy. Better income translates into more innovative management where experimentation is encouraged. There is tolerance for new ideas whose value is yet to be determined. When the coffers are full, every new idea gets some consideration and the best of the best get the funding that they need to develop into full-scale programs. Research and development thrive in times of plenty, and this is the case in nonprofits, too.

When times get hard, management moves into a control mode, cutting costs and focusing employees onto strict tasks and away from innovation activities such as exploration. Eliminating noncore duties and staff kills innovation for years to come. The chilling effects of a layoff are profound. Those that are not cut consider exactly what their role is and retrench themselves into their daily tasks in an attempt to prove to their supervisor that they are "doing their job." We have seen it with a number of organizations we have worked with and for. Actions such as these stifle the new idea pipeline and damage the culture for years to come.

Even in hard economic times never forget to reinforce the external value that your internal entrepreneurs bring beyond their work. Call attention to their efforts on your website, in newsletters, and in presentations. Use free public opportunities to laud their efforts and make them feel valued. In the unfortunate case you have to let them go, they will know their efforts were valued and leave with an amazing innovative record to show in their next interview.

Assessing Innovation in Potential Candidates

You are probably thinking if innovation sometimes defies prior expertise, how do we hire to that? Simple—assess the potential ability to drive innovation if your candidates lack prior direct innovation experience. More often than not, your candidates will not have formal innovation development experience on their resumes, so look for the potential in everyone. Look for complimentary attributes like general inquisitiveness, a desire to understand how things work, and an interest in entrepreneurial activities. Innovators may have clues in their resume and experience like taking initiative to drive change in an organization, a willingness to take on leadership roles, and the ability to tell you about the lessons they learned from failed projects in the past. The ability to innovate should be on the characteristics list for every position you hire at your nonprofit and anyone you recruit to your board, not just required of leadership positions.

You can test for innovation in people you hire. Here are two ways we assess and hire innovative people in organizations.

Ask Them Direct Questions. Duh. Seems simple, huh? But just do it. Actually include a question on innovation and futuring as a part of all the standard questions you ask candidates. Even the lowest-paying position at your nonprofit should have the shot to be in a leadership position someday. So test them. Ask them hard questions. Not just about how they handle fundraising and volunteers and working weekends. Ask them what the hardest thing was at their old/current job and how they innovated to solve the problem. Did they research, brainstorm with others, meditate about it? If they hem and haw you may want to add them to the skip list.

- We have been asked questions about innovation in job interviews, and have asked them of candidates as well. Some samples include: Tell me about your favorite piece of technology from Star Wars, Star Trek, Dr. Who, or some other science fiction property—even a video game! Then ask why and when they think it will be a reality.

- Ask about the coolest new technology or software development they heard about in the news recently. This tests their interest in current affairs and awareness of technology developments.
- Also ask them about their favorite thing to do on the Internet—and then ask them to give two suggestions to make that experience better.
- Inquire about a failed project from their work history and what they learned from the experience. Follow up by asking for a tangible example of how they used what they learned in another project.
- Look for eagerness to take on accountability and drive something new that they can call their own. Ask them how they would design a project development program and listen for hints of entrepreneurship and rule breaking.

Challenge Them to Think Right Then and There. Give candidates a scenario they have to solve through innovation. We like to think of two angles on this. Ask them for one involving innovation to solve an issue around technology in the office, and the other should be about a real-world problem involving looking outside the organization and its traditional way of doing things.

In terms of the first scenario, we like our employees to bend rules when needed. Since we tend to hire more digital employees in our work, our internal question often involves defeating an IT firewall to get to a site that a volunteer is questioning them about. (Sorry, IT departments everywhere.) We ask them to do this because we agree with Tom Kelly of IDEO when he says, "You learn from people who break the rules."[1] This can also play as an ethical question in the interview process by testing if your interviewee is brazen or bashful about their ability to think and go around the rules.

The second scenario involves looking outside the organization to a problem your nonprofit has and how they should solve it.

---

[1]Tom Kelly, *The Art of Innovation* (Currency/Doubleday: New York, NY, 2001), p. 39.

This could be anything from how they might monitor thousands of mentions of your nonprofit in the blogosphere, to a specific issue that your volunteers want to solve. The idea is to put them on the spot and make them solve it. Be less concerned about their actual answer and more concerned about how they arrive at the answer. Let them talk through their thinking around solving the problem. Again, are they researching, evaluating, and testing ideas? Or did they go cowboy and decide on a course of action just because? Their approach tells you a lot about their personality and how well they will handle future challenges.

Follow Up On Their References

Tons of folks come through the hiring process and give supposedly great references but nonprofits get so wrapped up in paperwork, criminal background checks, and department buy-in when hiring people they seem to forget to take this really simple step. Actually make time on your calendar and call two of the three people that your applicant listed as references. Ask the references hard questions about the applicant and how they performed in their former organizations. Did they really have three employees and an intern working for them? How many volunteers did they really manage? How much contact did they really have with volunteers? Most importantly, ask if that person would hire your candidate to do the job they are interviewing for. A few other questions include:

1. Who else should I speak to about this person?
2. What contributions did they make to your organization?
3. Would you hire them back if the chance came up?
4. What are they best/worst at?
5. Why do you think they are leaving your organization?

Also, don't be afraid to look for other public information about your candidate on social media sites like LinkedIn and Facebook. Some people think that this is an invasion of privacy but we know that many times these spaces can be perfectly curated by the user to present the best that they have to offer. Before you go looking, just make sure you know what you are looking for and looking at. Judge them by the content they create and nothing more.

Five Points to Remember

In his book *The Art of the Start,* Guy Kawasaki says you have to "ignore the irrelevant" when hiring truly innovative people into your organization. He has a list of double edged swords to look for when hiring a candidate. In our opinion, these are very true and apply to recruiting leadership volunteers as well as paid staff. Five we'd like to showcase include:

Experience in a Successful Organization: How much did they really do to make success happen, or were they just along for the ride? Understanding direct contributions can give you a great sense of if the candidate is a leader, supporter, or a slacker.

Experience in a Failed Organization: How much did they learn from the failure? Ask about what they learned with regard to their work and the work of others. If they can tell you about the broad circumstances, then you know you have someone with a vision. Also be mindful if they communicate they are *always* at failed organizations.

Educational Background: Apple CEO Steve Jobs never finished Reed College. Filmmaker Robert Rodriguez took 10 years to finish the University of Texas at Austin. A famous physician once asked a crowd, "What do they call the guy who graduated dead last in his class from medical school? Doctor."

Experience in the Same Industry: Are they stuck in a rut and unable to break out of a mold? Or are they experts in this industry and staying because they know they have a lot to offer?

Experience in the Same Function: Selling phone book advertising is not the same as being a volunteer at a health organization. However, Ford Motor Company built the first car assembly line from people who worked in meatpacking and at breweries. In this regard, be very careful in putting too much emphasis on what they have done before and really think about their underlying skills. For instance, even though phone book advertising and volunteer health work seem so different, they are both rooted in relationship management

The Three Levels of Innovation

So now that you have hired an innovative employee at your nonprofit, how do we continue to build them into an innovative leader? Once again, we don't want to screen for innovation for its own sake. What we need to do is build leadership that recognizes the three levels of innovation in your nonprofit:

1. incremental
2. incremental with side effects, and
3. transformational.

You need to have leadership that is not scared to see these three things happen, and will promote them while concentrating on your day-to-day mission.

Interview: Capital Area Food Bank Makes Innovation Thrive

We spoke with Lisa Goddard, Advocacy and Online Marketing Director of the Capital Area Food Bank (CAFB), and she answered some questions we had about the environment at the CAFB in terms of innovation, support, staffing, and structure. This interview illuminates many things, one of which is how all three levels of innovation can work together at a nonprofit.

David and Randy: How and what innovations did you start at your current or past job?

Lisa: I have been providing digital marketing expertise to the Food Bank since August 2005. My relationship began with the Food Bank as an AmeriCorps VISTA volunteer. I was brought on staff in September 2006 where my time was split between advocacy/public policy work and online marketing. Since 2010, I only direct the Food Bank's digital marketing strategy where I supervise one staff person devoted to online development.

Prior to my relationship with the Food Bank, there was no online marketing staff, no formal email communication plan, and the 40-page-deep

website included one basic online donation
page. Today, the Food Bank's digital marketing
and communication efforts, which I lead include:
Facebook, Twitter, videos, podcasts, live streaming events, multiple websites and micro sites,
segmented and personalized email engagement,
an iPhone app, mobile messaging, online advocacy, and online donation management services.

Also, some notable digital marketing and communications
accomplishments during my tenure include:

- CAFB is the first food bank in the nation to have an iPhone
  app with more than 200 downloads in the first three months
  of launch.
- I was an *Austin-American-Statesman* Social Media Award recipient
  in 2009.
- Nearly 13 percent of the Food Bank's individual giving is
  through digital channels (recurring, one-time, and major
  gifts, and virtual food drives).
- I have implemented, grown, and managed an online community of nearly 44,000 hunger fighters.
- CAFB's email subscriber list has grown more than 60 percent
  two years in a row.
- CAFB's hungermaps project uses Google maps technology to
  provide rich content and context to hunger relief resources
  and the need in Central Texas.

David and Randy: How did the innovation effort get initiated?

Lisa: In 2006, I didn't micro blog in the way we
                   know micro blogging today, but used micro
                   blogging techniques on the CAFB website
                   during disaster relief for hurricane Katrina.
                   I designated a space on the CAFB home page
                   to "tweet" updates about most-needed dona-
                   tion items, volunteer opportunities, and thank
                   yous for in-kind donations.
                       Further, as the need for hunger relief grew in
                   Central Texas, and the organization brought on

additional staff and a new president and CEO in 2008, I recognized an opportunity to ramp up digital communication beyond monthly e-newsletters and action alerts. The social media resources available at that time supported the capacity and talent within the organization, and the Food Bank's new leadership embraced social media, especially blogging. It was time to innovate and for me to lead the organization's social media efforts.

CAFB's blog is an initiative to share the Food Bank's impact and total value to the community and stakeholders without compromising the action-oriented design and site architecture of austinfoodbank.org. Twitter provides the community with person-to-person interaction with staff—the Food Bank's greatest ambassadors and embodiments of the mission. Mobile messaging, iPheedANeed iPhone app, podcasts, and other initiatives were developed to further help the community understand the hunger crisis.

Social media has made me a powerful anti-hunger evangelist and I believe it has done the same for many others. The Tyson Foods relationship, which started through a tweet introduction (a tweetroduction, if you will) by you, David, provided many fun Twitter, video, and blogging projects while helping to raise awareness, food, and funds for the Food Bank.

The Austin Food Bloggers Hunger Awareness project is another great example of how I use social media to support and showcase the great ideas and passion from our community. Through the help of Kristi Willis and Addie Broyles, long-time food bank supporters and food bloggers, I shared 73 stories from local bloggers who cooked and ate from a typical offering from a food pantry for one week.

David and Randy: Do you have executive support for your efforts?

Lisa: Yes! The Food Bank's very first blog posts were authored by former president and chief executive officer David Davenport when he shared his Food Stamp challenge experience, eating on a dollar-a-meal budget for the month. His contributions inspired the Hunger is UNacceptable photo gallery on Flickr (more than 100 people contributed photos to build the gallery during the month-long promotion) and eventually CAFB's awareness campaign of the same name. He's an avid tweeter (@Ddavenport) and a regular blog author.

David and Randy: How is your role/department structured? Does it give you more freedom to experiment with new ideas and concepts?

Lisa: Online marketing is part of the Mobilizing Communities team, which consists of Advocacy and Public Policy, Resource Development, Community Events, and Marketing and Branding. As Online Marketing Director, I supervise one person who is responsible for the organization's online development and fundraising goals. My direct manager is responsible for all marketing, communications, and branding. I do have freedom to experiment with new ideas and concepts. Many of those ideas come through the scheduled brainstorming meetings I lead, through digital communication trainings I conduct internally, and by participating in cross-departmental meetings. I also use a variety of project management tools to document processes and stay organized. All of these combined creates a fertile ground for creativity and inspiration.

David and Randy: What are your requirements before you invest time and money into a new project?

Lisa:
First and foremost, the project must support the mission. If the project doesn't help nourish the hungry and lead the community in ending hunger, then it is not providing proper stewardship to the community.

Second, the project should support the strategic plan, the short- and long-term goals of the organization, and the team goals.

Third, the project must produce results. Quantifiable measures such as dollars, or new email addresses are important, but so is learning. I seek to understand what potential and current constituents are seeing when looking for information online, whether it's about the Food Bank, or something the Food Bank can offer. I want to know what they are doing when they find the Food Bank's information. I want to know what they are saying about the Food Bank and receive feedback easily. Every new digital project should substantially and uniquely help CAFB understand the community it serves. Digital projects are approached with a sincere desire to improve the Food Bank's relationship with individuals in the community and provide value.

Fourth, I evaluate how the project may impact other team members in the organization. A silo approach to digital projects is not sustainable; more often than not, a digital project affects other departments within the organization. Having preliminary conversations about digital projects with other departments not only develops trust and provides buy-in for a project, but also provides me with a realistic understanding of a project's timing and coordination requirements.

David and Randy:
What is your success/failure rate?

Lisa:
The Austin Reggae Festival mobile messaging is a great example of success within failure. The

Mobilizing Communities team spent months promoting the four-digit short code for the three-day festival. Hours before the festival began, technical issues beyond the Food Bank's control caused the short code to disappear, and a seven-digit number was used for the rest of our campaign. While it wasn't an ideal situation to say the least, I was able to accomplish several goals I outlined which included getting more new constituents. Through the mobile messaging project, CAFB connected with nearly 2,000 constituents, 60 percent of whom were new to the CAFB online community. But success measurement doesn't end with the digital marketing tool usage. The next chapter is to thank and introduce the new constituents to the Food Bank's mission, services, and opportunities to volunteer, advocate, and donate. This is why with a new project, especially involving ever-evolving digital technologies, intelligence gathering must be part of the objective and goals. With ever-changing digital technology, you cannot let inabilities interfere or derail you from what you can do. It's what you learn and put into practice after your project that really matters.

David and Randy: What is the most valuable thing you have learned both tactically and strategically?

Lisa: Spend time planning and brainstorming before plunging in. It's the little things that allow big things to happen and provide those opportunities for serendipity. A good plan will expose opportunity for cross-organizational involvement and disaster management.

Don't do too much at once. Most of all, you can't outsource organizational expertise and passion for your organization. Your agency or consultant may have an understanding of best practices, and how a particular piece of technology works, but don't mistake that for expertise on your constituents, organizational strategy, and mission.

Also, social media has transformed the way the team thinks about return on investment. In traditional communication channels, "share of mind," impressions delivered, and other one-to-one measurement models are used for evaluation. Social media supports a holistic way of interacting with the world around us. I'm constantly thinking about how I can use social media tools to deliver great content in a way that is adaptable, supports interaction, sharing, and manipulation. Ultimately, it's about helping a network of supporters bring hunger issues to the forefront and providing the opportunity for hunger issues to be communicated in many ways—even ways in which we have little control. The mediums chosen must be varied, as specific demographics, particularly young adults and teens, grow weary of certain aspects of social media. Facebook use is decreasing among young adults and teens, and teens are not big on tweeting. However, mobile use is going through the roof with this demographic. In a few years, this may not be the case. Any digital marketing strategy I implement must be flexible enough so I don't have to start from scratch every time a hot new social media tool is on the scene. Think of it as nomadic marketing communications for the digital world. If I'm using social media correctly, by providing compelling content, communicating with respect, and demonstrating leadership, the hunger issues will naturally bubble up to the surface of consciousness and will organically weave into the everyday conversations of Central Texans at home, at work, online, and everything in-between.

David and Randy: And what is the most important reason to continue funding your innovation effort?

Lisa: The innovations I've helped the organization
                         develop have proven success through a growing
                         base of supporters, the community's deeper
                         involvement with our efforts, and understanding
                         of hunger in Central Texas.

Growing an Innovative Employee into Something More

Incremental innovation is defined by Douglas Merrill, CIO of Google,
as "evolution, the process of animals and plants adapting to their
unique environments over time."[2] He also gives an example of an
incremental innovation with side effects as, "consider the opposable
thumb . . . the fact of one more finger shifting in the human species suddenly allowed us to use tools." Although simplifying, he has
an amazing point. Tool use because of the side effect of having an
opposable thumb allowed the human species to build civilization
into what it is today. Evolutionarily, this was not a huge change.
We simply evolved into having another finger which gave us the
ability to use tools and reap the advantages of the tools.

Transformative change is hard to find in biology but it is not
hard to find in business. A great example of transformative change
in business is Gmail. Google is a search and advertising company.
However, as we mentioned before, one of their most transformative
innovations has been Gmail, which was invented by a Google engineer
because of Google's 20 percent rule: Google encourages engineers to
spend a day a week on projects that interest them and are unrelated
to their day jobs. "If a Google user has a problem with email, well, so
do we," said Google co-founder and president of technology, Sergey
Brin. "And while developing Gmail was a bit more complicated than
we anticipated, we're pleased to be able to offer it to the user who
asked for it."[3]

Gmail has well over a hundred million unique visitors every
month. There are millions of nonprofits, people, and organizations
that depend on their free email service, even though they are orig-
inally a search and advertising provider. That is a transformative

---

[2]http://www.youtube.com/watch?v=2GtgSkmDnbQ
[3]http://www.google.com/press/pressrel/gmail.html. According to Jessica
Vascellaro, Feb. 8, 2010

innovation in the way that Google does business. Of course it helps Google's bottom line that it is actively scanning all emails to provide targeted ads on the side of every Gmail account page, which, in turn, they sell to advertisers. As Tom Davenport, a senior lecturer at Harvard, says, "It doesn't matter if you are an economist, a programmer, or a senior search researcher . . . at Google the best idea wins."[4] Again, though, Gmail departed so drastically from the core business models of "Google, the advertising company." Free email was not a core competency or function of an advertising company, but Google took the challenge on and created a transformative piece of technology. Their efforts in the space drove substantial value to their customers, and to the company as a whole. Overall, the way Gmail was developed was incremental but the value it drove to the consumer was incremental with great side effects, and the business model that Gmail finally delivered was truly transformative.

For all three of these types of innovation you need leadership that understands, encourages, and develops them. This fact needs to be something that you rate and judge all employees on, no matter their role in the nonprofit. By doing this every year, for every employee, you can really start to create a baseline of innovation in your nonprofit, especially as you incorporate this as something that all managers have to grade and score their employees on.

No Aspect Is Too Small

We just wanted to mention something that might seem obvious but a lot of times gets swept under the rug: The fact that many traditional nonprofits jokingly and lovingly call anyone that is supporting office tasks—like people in HR, administration, finance, or information technology—"overhead employees." Basically "overhead" in NPOs is all-too-often considered anything that doesn't directly serve a client. In any basic agency setting, when there is a service provided, the agency often becomes divided: client services versus nondirect client services. Therefore, if you do not directly serve clients, you are seen as "overhead."

---

[4]http://www.youtube.com/watch?v=QOioQxtJ4gI&NR=1&feature=fvwp

To quote Narissa Johnson, of Southwest Key in Austin, Texas:

> "The challenge is, without things like marketing, advertising, IT, and air-conditioning in a warehouse (in Texas!), etc., direct and nondirect client services can't get done. I have had an ED say to me that she hates to spend money on things that aren't going to clients during a discussion about the fact that the IT infrastructure hadn't been updated in a decade and was falling apart!
>
> I think until NPOs stop viewing 'overhead' as a necessary evil that they rue spending money on, they will continue to get the small slice of this pie everyone keeps referring to . . . and more importantly, will never create actual change around the issues they claim to seek change around."

We agree with her. The usual metrics used in evaluations—what you rate and grade your employees on from volunteer recruitment to press release writing to meeting fundraising goals and beyond—need to include innovation-minded questions and forward-thinking exercises. Including them will guarantee that each employee thinks about his/her own progress and acing their evaluations.

Even nonforward-thinking managers should be ready to present a challenge. Helping managers understand what should be evaluated as innovation ensures that everyone is being evaluated fairly, and that everyone is driving real tangible value back to the organization. You are going to get what you measure, so be sure that everyone sees the value and understands the metrics clearly.

From our interview with John Kenyon, Nonprofit Technology Educator and Strategist

"When beginning an engagement, I assess the support of the ED and the Board for the initiative. If the executives don't understand why they need to be effective online, they can doom a project. Since many nonprofit Boards are made up of people over 50, for whom technology is often not a strength, they often need education and guidance in this area, which they can be loath to request. When there is support, it creates an atmosphere where experiments are possible and innovation can thrive."

There will always be managers that fail to see the value in innovation and are uncooperative in evaluating and rewarding innovative thinking. In cases like these, though, it's time to hire new managers.

Conclusion

Staffing is the most critical component of an innovation program. Even if you have the right approach and culture for awareness, and you have a structure that allows for quick and effective innovation development, if you lack the staff to execute all the things within those areas, you are fighting an uphill battle.

Organizations need to identify the innovation-capable talent they have, and recruit more talent for the future. It is important to engage and involve the human resources department and board of directors early and often. Help them understand the importance and value of innovation in general and the attributes that they need to recruit for. Help them leverage nontraditional sources of talent such as online communities, local technology club chapters, and advisory volunteers.

The most innovative companies in the world all share the same thing: outstanding staff. IDEO, Google, Design Forum . . . they all recruit, manage, and retain talent that is intelligent and flexible. Hiring innovative minds means you should also have a plan to leverage them, too. It is as important as acquiring them.

Whether you are working in a nationwide organization or a small local nonprofit, the reality is that you are in competition with the top for-profit companies around for top talent and top volunteers. One way to attract them is to have a plan to develop and retain them over the long haul. This is an important key to having a great nonprofit.

IMPLEMENTATION AND FUTURE CONSIDERATIONS

CHAPTER

8

Starting Your Innovation Projects

MANAGING INNOVATION
AT YOUR ORGANIZATION

An object at rest stays at rest and an object in motion stays in motion.

—Sir Isaac Newton

ewton's first law should help spur us into action at the outset of this chapter because it aims to give you the energy you need to set your innovation effort in motion.

To get started, take a look at your staff, find the rule breakers, and begin to initiate a Skunkworks effort. The term Skunkworks originated in the Lockheed Martin Advanced Development Programs department. It is used to describe an internal group (either a project team or special department) that is given a range of freedom not given to the rest of the organization. Skunkworks often work on special projects that require them to operate outside of the bounds of the traditional organization.

Why do organizations do this? Because the typical way of doing things produces typical work and a Skunkworks program is charged with producing *atypical* work—innovative and leading-edge work that can only be done in an unencumbered working environment.

We bring up the concept of Skunkworks because this chapter is about bootstrapping an innovation project together from little to no resources. Bootstrapping is starting a business concept from zero, with no external help. If you are preparing to bootstrap you may have to beg, borrow, and steal time, energy, and resources to get your concept off the ground. In this kind of environment, you'll need advice on how to kick off an innovation program in your organization, and how to actually create the thing from scratch and get it running.

Since there is a very good chance that you will be creating your innovation program from the ground up, we will give you advice from our experience in start-ups as well as offer you a first-hand look at how we were a part of the establishment of an internal Futuring and Innovation Center at a nonprofit. By the end of the chapter, we want to have inspired you, given you tactical steps on how to start your own innovation program, and provided you with some guidance on what a well-running innovation program looks like.

How to Ignite Innovative Projects

So far, we have covered the three components of successful innovation: awareness, structure, and staffing. We have given you examples and suggestions on refocusing your goals and objectives in order to be a more innovative organization.

To really drive an innovation project, you need to inspire your innovative employees. Employing creative and dedicated employees who will donate their energy and effort above and beyond their regular 9 to 5 hours is key. Their input, their buy-in, and their dedication to the vision of a better organization are all going to be the driving force that makes your vision a reality. To be really successful in developing an innovation program you have to be presenting a great alternative to the current way of doing things. You need to be able to define value and, frankly, the best way to do this is to look at the old way of doing and developing ideas and comparing it to how it could be.

The Old Way

Before we get to the operations of a Skunkworks, think about how you collect and funnel new ideas right now. Again, is it a boring and tired idea box in the hallway (see Figure 8.1)?

Figure 8.1   Suggestion Box
Source: http://www.flickr.com/photos/mskogly/2381707051/, http://creativecommons.
org/licenses/by/2.0/deed.en.
Photo by Morten Skogly, Creative Commons Licensed

Is it a small note at the bottom of your monthly internal newsletter (right after the monthly cafeteria menu) that asks employees for new ideas? Look at new ideas and how many you are actually getting. If you think the reason you aren't getting ideas is because you are doing everything right, we can immediately tell you one thing we know you are doing wrong! Everyone likes to see solutions. Next, we lay out how you can drive innovation under the radar, out of bounds, and in the rough where you'll have the flexibility to take on small challenges and systematically solve problems.

The New Way

John Kenyon, Nonprofit Technology Educator & Strategist, told us his key to driving innovation under the radar in an interview:

> "Innovation cannot happen in a vacuum in my experience. It is
> the result of continually learning, listening to the experiences and
> advice of others, then weaving those together to create new ideas
> and concepts. Sometimes it is just putting two disparate things
> together in the right way that creates something new. Other times,
> the right juxtaposition of two seemingly opposite or contradictory
> ideas can help both be seen in a new light. Like art often does, it
> helps people find new ways to see themselves and their worlds.
>
> I generate new ideas and concepts on the shoulders of and
> based on input from generous colleagues and others who share
> their ideas, experiences, disappointments, and successes."

Further, we would like to add to this some detail on advice (which we mentioned earlier in the book) we'd gotten from Mike Mitchell, of the American Cancer Society (ACS): "Don't just post a box in the hallway. Start a systematic approach to attracting and finding breakthrough innovation ideas." As we said, we touched on this before, but Mike's is a very important strategy: Ask people what they think, do it in a new way, and ask them in a way that will make their feedback take you in a positive direction.

Mike's approach started a "suggestion box" that lived on the ACS Intranet and external website. This wasn't just a "What's wrong?" box. Instead Mike positioned this online form as an opportunity box and it asked, "What can we do better?"

He developed an ingenious way to maximize the ideas that came into this idea funnel. He worked through the evaluation process to assign each idea a path. Some ideas were simply banked and saved for future reference. When an idea was banked the innovation team made sure to document the reason why: Perhaps it would not scale, it lacked a measurable mission, or a similar idea had been tried and failed. Some ideas that were banked included major capital expenses, hyper-local concepts that leveraged niche cultural trends, even making staff drive around with magnetic signs on their cars and other concepts that did not fit the organization's image.

By sifting through the ideas in a systematic way, Mike realized that some of them, while amazing, were not destined for full development. Instead of just discarding them and placing them in the historical record, he passed the ideas on to various department heads and managers as pieces of inspiration. The concept of using a flash mosaic of individual donors' photos for a tribute program was not quite breakthrough enough for the innovation program, but it was deftly incorporated into an existing program in another department and really enhanced it. This idea in particular became ACS's Mosaic of Memories.[1]

The best ideas were moved on to final reviews, funding, and prototyping. Over the course of four years, about 5 percent of the ideas they received went forward to development funding. Of those, they prototyped 13 marketing programs, all of them ahead of their

---

[1]www.cancer.org/involved/donate/personalfundraising/mosaic

time—produced in less than 18 months—and for under $35,000. Some of them were monumental successes. What Mike and eventually the other executives involved in ASC's Innovation Center at the time realized was that the more people you had contributing, the more effective the innovation effort was.

Mike was also highly influenced by the Shell Game Changer program[2] and how it operated. He developed a multi-stage process designed to evaluate and screen ideas based on their potential value to the organization, and then align resources to give that idea the support it needed to materialize. The idea of throwing out a wide net to bring in and evaluate as many ideas as possible was the backbone of his strategy. It was that rigorous review process that transformed the "suggestion box" into a generator of great ideas and eventually great products and projects.

Mike's Model Innovation Process. The innovation review process Mike used has five steps. We both have lived and worked through this process for years and we know that it works. It delivers real value to organizations of any size. As both product innovators and corporate innovation reviewers, we know that in order to innovate, you need a strong structure through which you review your nonprofit's ideas. We touched on this process before in Chapter 6, but we are going to hit the five points again—as Mike implemented them—here.

- Step #1: Intake: Gather submitted business concept descriptions via any means necessary on a targeted organizational challenge. Throw the widest possible net to capture as many ideas as possible.
- Step #2: First Review: Give the concept an initial review against its funding criteria: Scalability, Sustainability, Cost Basis, Tie to Organizational Mission, Capacity for Execution.
- Step #3: Business Case: The submitter is paired with a mentor from the review team. Together they create a business plan which is thoroughly evaluated based on a prototype scale. The business plan is the formal application for funding. The mentor

---

[2] www.shell.com/home/content/innovation/bright_ideas/game_changer

presents the business plan to the overall idea team and serves as liaison during the funding consideration discussions.

- Step #4: Development and Testing: The submitter receives funding and support to create a rapid prototype to prove their concept within 18 months. Funding is based on the business plan budget with an upper limit of $25,000. The mentor and the idea team work with the submitter to provide feedback no less frequently than each quarter. Upon completion of the rapid prototype process the idea team reviews the final outcomes.
- Step #5: Launch: If chosen for implementation, the idea team, the submitter, and national leadership identify the department best suited to deliver the program to market, and arrange a smooth transition and success of the new program.

You may be thinking that you have to work in a large organization to be able to initiate an innovation program. Not so. Small organizations are also starting executive innovation projects across the nation. They are thinking outside of their traditional organizational boundaries and delivering projects and programs that are impacting their mission on limited resources.

Interview: Meals on Wheels and More

Meals on Wheels and More (MOWAM) is a local Austin, Texas, nonprofit. Their mission is to nourish and enrich the lives of the homebound and other people in need through programs that promote dignity and independent living in Central Texas.

In 2010, MOWAM celebrated 38 years of service in the greater Austin area. What began as a program of eight volunteers serving 29 seniors has now expanded into a multi-service organization of 5,000 volunteers serving almost 3,400 elderly and disabled persons each day.

It's this mission that drove the latest innovative program from MOWAM: an Alzheimer's care center for East Austin called Mike's Place. We sat down with Sarah Andrews, MOWAM Director of Communications, to learn more.

David and Randy: Can you give us an example of a time when your organization initiated and launched a truly innovative project? What was it?

Sarah:

In February 2010, Meals on Wheels and More opened Mike's Place, a new activity center for individuals with Alzheimer's and dementia that simultaneously provides respite for their caregivers. The center is the first of its kind in East Austin. While there are several activity centers for individuals with Alzheimer's in Austin, most are located west of I-35, leaving East Austin-ites who are suffering from dementia and their caregivers without adequate local resources.

Currently, Mike's Place is a free service that is open from 9:30 A.M. to 1:30 P.M. on Wednesdays and from 10 A.M. to 2 P.M. on the second Saturday of the month.

David and Randy:

How did the idea come about?

Sarah:

Many of our employees at Meals on Wheels and More have been affected personally by the disease of Alzheimer's. Suellen Mills, our Vice President for Volunteer Services who has worked here for 38 years, is the primary caretaker for her husband Mike. Over the years, Mike has become a big part of the Meals on Wheels family and a friend to all who work here. Mike has spent a lot of time at our offices and was the primary inspiration for the center, which is named after him.

Marjorie Murphey Camacho, a geriatric care manager in our Client Services department and a registered nurse, was also the primary caretaker for her mother, who had Vascular Dementia and passed away this year. Also, Natalie Freeman, a 28-year-old newlywed who works in our Volunteer Services department, is the primary caretaker for her mother, Barbara, who also visits our offices frequently.

Because of the difficulties each of these women faced in finding suitable daycare for their loved ones that was convenient to our offices in East Austin, Suellen and Marjorie began discussing the need for a center in this part of town. As a social worker conducting home visits with our elderly clients in East Austin, Marjorie clearly saw a need for this kind of resource in the area. Many of our clients in East Austin who have dementia couldn't participate in West Austin activity centers because of transportation issues. We also saw that there were some perceived barriers to attaining these services due to cultural and socioeconomic differences.

The personal and professional familiarity Suellen and Marjorie have with Alzheimer's and working with the elderly population gave them the confidence to pursue the idea further with our CEO Dan Pruett and Vice President for Client Services Mary Teeters, who both supported the idea. Even though operating a center of this kind falls outside of our traditional service areas, our senior management team and board of directors didn't feel that we would be running the risk of "mission creep" because Mike's Place fit well with our expertise in serving the elderly and disabled in a holistic manner and because there was a clear need for a center of its kind in East Austin.

David and Randy: What were the obstacles and opportunities discovered in the development process?

Sarah: Money, staffing, and space were the initial barriers.

But in 2008, we began a building expansion project to accommodate the growth of our organization as we respond to the growing needs of an aging population in Austin. The expansion was necessary to increase the size of our kitchen and Client Services department so we can produce more meals and continue to provide holistic case management services to our clients. In addition to providing more than 1 million meals annually to Austin's home-bound, we also offer services through 11 "And More" programs that respond to the additional needs homebound individuals have, such as assis-tance getting to the grocery store and medical appointments, assistance with home repairs, and assistance caring for their pets.

With space opening up at our Central Kitchen headquarters, we began looking for funding for Mike's Place and secured a grant from the St. David's Foundation. With the support of St. David's we were able to make the necessary renovations to the existing space (i.e., put in a new restroom and make the area accessible for people with disabilities.) We also restructured the job responsibilities of Marjorie and Suellen so that they were freed up to oversee the opera-tion of Mike's Place. We then created a new volunteer program for people interested in assisting Mike's Place participants and leading group activities.

Another notable obstacle was finding par-ticipants. While there is a great need for adult daycare and caregiver respite in East Austin, we found that not many people in the area were actively seeking it out. Because of varying socio-economic factors, we found that many elderly East Austin-ites we served lacked a familiarity with the concept and instead relied solely on family for help. While researching the service models other centers in West and North Austin were using, we found that while participants and caregivers utilizing many other Austin centers were proactive about their participation, we would need to work and educate our parti-cipants and their caregivers on the benefits of these programs. To do this, we also had to develop a recruitment plan for participants.

David and Randy: What have you learned from the experience and how has that directly translated into a better organization?

Sarah: Across the board, our employees involved with taking Mike's Place from idea to reality say that they are surprised at how fun it is. Before opening Mike's Place, much time was spent on contingency planning for "worst case scenarios," as it is common for individuals with Alzheimer's to have behavioral issues and to wander off. But what our staff has learned is that there are so many people in our community and at Meals on Wheels and More that support the program and because the activities are well-planned and engaging, the participants remain focused and upbeat. Mike's Place has benefited our organization by infusing it with a new spirit and energy. On Wednesdays, the hallways are filled with music and all of our staff members can observe the participants dancing or playing volleyball.

Mike's Place also reinforces so many of the core values our organization believes in, such as providing innovative and holistic service and establishing a personal connection to the people on our services. While some of our "And More" programs may have evolved from a more pragmatic starting point, Mike's Place came from the personal passion so many members of our leadership team have for helping individuals with Alzheimer's and dementia and their caregivers and to see this work done. Plus, Mike's Place also fills a real gap in services in East Austin. If there had been a respite center like this in East Austin already, it is doubtful that we would have made this undertaking.

David and Randy: Was there a formal process involved? If not, would it have been more helpful to have one?

Sarah: Mike's Place evolved from informal conversations that led to a more formal research and development effort. We do not have a formal process in place at Meals on Wheels and More for employees to submit ideas for new programs. Our CEO Dan Pruett, however, maintains an open door policy with all employees and encourages idea exchanges on any and all ways to make our organization better. Under his leadership, several new programs have launched that have helped us better serve our clients. Because we maintain this kind of open dialogue and atmosphere internally, we don't really feel that a formal process would benefit us, though we can see how it might be necessary at larger organizations. (We have about one hundred employees.)

How to Staff Your Innovation Project

Even if you have an outstanding structure for bringing in and developing innovation, it takes a dedicated staff to run and manage it. Leadership for this kind of venture can come from the very top. Whoever takes on the not-so-glorious task of initiating an innovation program should be in a position where they can exert influence, navigate political channels, and offer protection to newly launched prototypes when necessary. If you need some direction on how to hire this person, look at Appendix 1 for the job description.

We learned from people like Mike Mitchell that, in order to pull off a Skunkworks project, a number of talented people from across the organization need to be involved. By assembling an innovation team with varied backgrounds from different parts of the organization, you will not only create a pool of intelligence, but you will also create a pool of political allies that advocate for innovation projects in their departments and regions. Using staff in this way is central to the success of almost every innovative program.

At the start of this chapter, we mentioned that you will have to beg, borrow, and steal, and we were being genuine.

- You may have to *beg* top leadership for some of their staff's time. Whether it be a few hours a month for a team meeting/conference call, or a three-day retreat, you are going to have to ask permission for their time.
- You will, of course, *borrow* their brains and make sure that when you return them you leave them better off than when you received them. Inspire the people who interact with your innovation program and send them back to their native department with executable ideas that will improve their daily work.
- And, finally, prepare to *steal* staff. There are going to be occasions where you need to expand your capacity and you know the perfect candidate—but they work in another department. Do not be afraid to go forward and steal them. Play the cards correctly so that your new acquisition delivers more value to more people. Make their old manager look like a champion for recognizing the opportunity and encouraging the move.

How to Fire Up Your Organization

Now that you have the blueprint to create a basic innovation program and a few ideas on how to use staff resources, it is time to fire up your organization. As if getting executive buy-in, setting up a structure, and recruiting key staff was not enough, now you need to fire up your entire organization and get them to understand the value of the innovation program. It is critical that you get them to suggest ways to innovate and improve performance, so we will concentrate on the micro-level of individual staff. We hired them in Chapter 8 for their internal entrepreneurship talent and here's how to make them work for you.

Get Public, Get Loud

Be prepared that the most probable limiting factor of the success of an innovation program is the lack of submissions to the program. This almost always comes back to a general lack of knowledge about the program in the organization. Regardless of the size of the organization, it is exceptionally difficult to get in front of staff and stakeholders on a daily basis, especially during the infancy of the programs being innovated within (when they are first launched and developed). To be successful, you have to use *whatever means necessary* to engage as many people as possible to bring in as many ideas as you can.

Your success may not hinge on the quality of your work, the impact your innovations have on the mission, or the money that you raise. Your longevity hinges on the political support that you garner and the interest that you attract. Do not take the opportunity to overlook your needs and turn your eye away from self promotion.

As a rule of thumb strive to produce some kind of a white paper or a trend report to showcase your work in awareness at least every other month. Make sure that as you write and consider the content that you shape it to answer questions that you know your colleagues have. Use this opportunity to engage other minds within your nonprofit organization (NPO)—ask them to research and write the papers. This gets them interested, gets wide organizational recognition, and lightens the workload that falls on you.

Grab a Strong Task Force

As we've said, you can't go it alone to get ideas vetted and funded. You need to rely on a strong team of leaders from all over your organization, and if you are a small nonprofit then you need to rely on strong volunteers. The best way to organize is by forming an innovation task force. This is a group of folks that will help you vet and move ideas through stages. We recommend a good mix of folks from the following positions and departments.

- The Chief Operating Officer: The strength of his or her knowledge of the organization and business strategy will help guide projects.
- Human Resources: All projects flow through this department in some way or another. Grab an entry-level staff member from this department for fresh insights.
- Information Technology (IT): Bring in a senior-level manager from IT who has done things you admire and invite them to join. Having IT at the table from the start will help your project fly through technical requirements and feasible scenarios.

- Fundraising/Development: Invite a mid-level fundraising person to weigh in on projects. You know who earns the money to pay the bills so get them involved early.
- Communications: Instead of inviting your legal team, invite your mid-level communications manager. They will maintain an eye for branding, logo usage, and message positioning in a less formal way than a lawyer might.

If your nonprofit doesn't have some of these exact people in terms of titles/positions, that's okay. We are sure you have a similar organizational chart that you can pull from. The important thing to remember is to make sure it's a diverse team of staff or volunteers and rotate them around every two years. Also make sure this team meets once a month to discuss new idea submissions and the market, taking into account future casting ideas.

Award and Encourage

Create an award that you and your innovation task force can give out to people who have submitted ideas to your group, regardless of if you fund them or not. If you recognize participation publicly, you create awareness and raise the level of interest. People want to win awards so give them that opportunity to express their creative ideas as well as get excited about your effort.

Most importantly, celebrate your innovators. Whether you give grant funds or simply empower individuals to pursue their ideas, publicly celebrate them. Their success is your success, and our experience is that those individuals who are innovators not only get attention but also promotions and additional responsibilities. Maintain relationships with them even after their innovation has launched and run its course because they will be your allies in the near and long-term future.

Rules for Rule Breakers

In his book *Art of the Start*, Guy Kawasaki talks about the "internal entrepreneur." It is a tectonic shift for most nonprofit folks to think of themselves as entrepreneurs, much less internal ones. The typical mindset is that they are just there, slaving away for the cause or the greater good of the issue. However, after reading this book, you know these new people you have hired or promoted will not be feeling that way.

Your employees will hopefully be thinking, "How do I accomplish this goal, how do I solve this problem, and how do I use the technology that I know how to use to get it done?" Encourage them when they do well and correct problems with them when they arise, not six months later at a performance review. Most of all have patience with them, confidence in them, and give internal entrepreneurs encouragement and tangible support.

Between authors like Guy Kawasaki and Wayne M. Bundy, Ph.D., and our combined 20 years in nonprofits, we have come up with six internal recommendations for the innovators you are working with in your organization. These are our "rules for rule breakers" to inspire confidence and give support.

1. Find Your Samurai: Much as great swordsmen studied at the feet of great samurai in feudal Japan, you too need to find a great leader, or assign one to drive innovation projects. You need someone who is respected at the nonprofit, who rises above the politics, and is held in great respect; someone that internal entrepreneurs can turn to when they are having problems getting things done with their bosses, the board, or volunteers. This person need not be a contrarian, but rather, someone who can provide sage tactical advice, connect your innovators with the people that matter, and move the marble when it's needed. (This person could be on the task force we talked about or outside of that system if needed. For us, this was Mike Mitchell.)

2. Stay Under the Radar: "The new always look so puny—so unpromising—next to the reality of the massive, ongoing business," says Peter F. Drucker from the 1985 book *Innovation and Entrepreneurship*. So let's not invite people to look, shall we? Keep your innovation team members doing good work and be sure to tell people about their accomplishments and successes but don't cause trouble. Innovation prototypes are not the stuff of huge showcases for the board just yet. Keep it nice and tidy and involve who you need to, but don't go too far away from home base just yet. As Kawasaki says, "The higher you go at a company, the less people are going to (or *want* to) understand what you are doing."

3. Don't forget to Dance with Who Brought You: Make sure this project or program is not built around catapulting you out of the nonprofit to something bigger. Don't lose sight of what your primary goal is: Solving a problem or issue for the nonprofit you work for in a new way. We know that when you are getting close to releasing the new idea or program you will feel a wave of excitement in epic proportions (either people cheering you on in the organization or people wanting to woo you away). However, don't lose sight of the reason you went to work for a nonprofit in the first place.

4. Let the Man Find You: Something that we learned working at a large organization is that it's easy to have people say no. No is a much easier word than yes. (It is 30 percent shorter!) That being said, it's not always smart to go ask your boss's boss or executive director to approve every aspect of your project. This should be one of your last steps. Not that you hide information or steps from your managers, but remember rule #2. The higher up in the management chain the more you want them to find your project, approach you, and later on support it when the time is right. In other words: Don't find them, let them find you.

5. Manage the End of the Project: Even the most innovative project must have an end. Once your prototype is finished, launched, and evaluated where do you go? Does the internal entrepreneur go back to what they were doing? Do they start a new program? Do they measure the return on investment (ROI) and ride off into the sunset? Also, where does the program live? When David was finishing up SharingHope. TV, there was a lot of discussion about where the program should actually live. Was it a communications project, a fundraiser, or something else? The website was up, traffic was coming in, and videos were being uploaded. However, instead of continuing as a project manager and leader on SharingHope.TV, David went back to his normal job. During that time it was put on a shelf for six months while the national communications department decided where it belonged. SharingHope.TV was a user-generated content portal designed to provide inspiration and a space for cancer survivors to talk to other cancer survivors. Eventually

the project was kept independent and lives on its own Web property. However the relevance of it is in question, as it was never promoted, and has no internal entrepreneur driving it. So what is the best thing to do when the project is done? There must be a clear path in your nonprofit if you are to avoid this situation.

6. Find the Rule Breakers: In his book *The Art of Innovation* Tom Kelly talks about finding rule breakers: "People who follow directions perfectly and can't imagine a different course aren't much help. You learn more from a woman who takes a shortcut, who forces the product to do something it says it can't, who imagines what it might do if only ..." Finding rule breakers is a key rule because identifying them early gives you the ability to cultivate their talent and harness their creativity. If you see a rule breaker ask them what inspired them to devise their solution and then challenge them to solve other problems. No one learns anything new by doing the same old thing and following the rules. We learn from rule breakers.

Our Challenge to You

Managing and creating the *right group in the right way* is going to drive success to your nonprofit Skunkworks innovation effort. In his book, *The Art of Discovery*, Wayne M. Bundy, Ph.D., writes: "the three most important goals of a ... group are a) discovery, b) new product ideas, and c) help in the transition of new ideas into profit." If we look at this with a nonprofit lens those three points would become: a) innovation, b) new service ideas and programs, and c) help in transitioning new ideas into new programs and services.

To make these three things happen in your nonprofit, here is our full list of recommendations of things to do and goals to strive for. We like to think that this would be a great list to have posted in the hallway at your workplace:

1. Promote a highly interactive knowledge-based system through a lab structure.
2. Enforce a judicious balance between time used for innovation and time used for other tasks (see Google's famous "20 percent time.")

3. Promote the study of anomalies, aid the success of projects, and dare all people to be the best in their fields.
4. Promote a mood of pristine honesty and freedom to express ideas.
5. Support the needs of incubation—more than one task and intense study followed by a respite from the problem in question.
6. Promote diverse strategic research to address the weakest links in the understanding of critical problems.
7. Promote the air of wide-ranging thought, using some thought methods outside the bounds of the routine.
8. Assert the value of knowledge exchange both in and outside the company.
9. Reward all idea growth and make certain the best ideas are tested.
10. Promote intrinsic drive and help people to control their future.
11. Sell to management the conviction that all people taking part in discovery must be honored in order for the process to flourish.

Out of those 11, we can further narrow it down to fit the top five that apply to nonprofit organizations. Here, we've reworked the top five concepts for maximum flow in a nonprofit system. If you are going to dedicate yourselves to only five points, please focus your energy here:

1. Give staff back their time. Enforce the idea that a certain percentage each week of their time is used for creative/innovative thinking.
2. Support the needs of incubation: Intense study of a program or service followed by a respite from the issue in question.
3. Promote a culture of strategic research among staff and volunteers. Organize and encourage the wisdom of the crowds inside and outside your nonprofit.
4. Reward all idea growth, and make certain that the best ideas are tested.
5. From the top to the bottom of your nonprofit, make sure that everyone involved in innovation is rewarded if you want the process to flourish and take root.

Conclusion

Managing and creating programs to promote innovation is hard work, and getting started is often the hardest part. There are great ways to leverage the best that your organization has to offer and make it drive value to your constituents both day in and day out.

Remember that you do not have to be in a large organization to get innovation projects going. No matter your organization's size, it is important to start out small and build a critical mass. Beg, borrow, and steal resources and use those resources to provide more value than anyone else thought possible. To recap:

- Do your best to get a formal structure set up for attracting, evaluating, and driving innovation projects forward.
- Work outside of the lines if you have to, and remember Skunkworks projects give you freedom because they are ultimately driving value.
- And when you have small victories, celebrate them openly and use them as recruiting tools to get more people excited about your work. Once you have victories, they will draw people to you and get them motivated and excited about the project, compounding your enthusiasm and combining energy to drive the project forward.

We would love to see how different types of people in different organizations start their innovation programs. Please keep us in the loop, and let us know how we can help, by visiting our Facebook page and leaving us a message. Or, you can join our mailing list and engage in further discussion by visiting our website at www .thefutureofnonprofits.com.

Next up, we'll offer our ideas on the future of NPO fundraising.

The Future of Fundraising

NEW MONEY FROM NEW DONORS
IN NEW WAYS

*Moving forward, fundraisers will need to become more sophisticated
in combining both traditional channels and new media while also
investing in the proper tools and resources to ensure all fundraising
programs are truly integrated and meet the ever-changing
communication preferences of donors.*
—Vinay Bhagat, Chief Strategy Officer, Convio

We tend to expect that when the future happens, it will be
accompanied with great fanfare to herald its arrival. The truth is
that the future subtly establishes itself bit by bit and it is our job to
continuously look for it in everyday incremental advancements.
We have both had ah-ha moments when working on projects or
reading articles wherein we instantly recognized the potential of
a current idea branching out into bigger and better future uses
and possibilities. When we saw Second Life, we saw the future of
community-based fundraising. When we saw Wikipedia, we saw the
future acceptance of user-generated content. It simply takes vision
and awareness to see the future of fundraising in today's projects and
programs.

Predicting the future can be a scary thing for nonprofits and
the scariest part of it can be thinking about where, who, and how

they will receive funding in the future to continue their missions. Will funding come in the form of grants, traditional event revenue, donations, or something more radical? For large nonprofits, here is some even scarier news: The *Chronicle of Philanthropy* reported in October of 2010 that donations to the nation's largest charities dropped 11 percent last year.

The *Chronicle* called this the worst decline in giving in 20 years. The median expected change for nonprofits in 2010 was supposed to be an increase of 1.4 percent. Instead, so far in 2010, giving to the United Way Worldwide (the largest charity in the survey) decreased by 4.5 percent and giving to Salvation Army (the second largest charity in the survey) dropped by 8.4 percent. Further, donations to the American Cancer Society dropped by a shocking 11 percent. Part of relying on a continued income stream is creating a future cast of your organization. As we discussed in prior chapters, creating a future cast helps you plan ideal goals toward which you can drive your organization.

By using awareness scanning techniques, we realize one of the most important trends from the last few years is online fundraising. Online fundraising is one of the most rapidly growing ways that nonprofits receive funds from individuals. In the third quarter of 2009, giving was up 41 percent compared to in the same time a year prior, and the trend toward giving online continues.[1]

This is interesting when taken alongside the information from the *Chronicle*. Even though giving overall has decreased at large nonprofits, across the board online giving is up in 2010 over 2009 in all sizes of nonprofits (whether large, medium, or small). Blackbaud—a leading online giving software company—reported that large organizations (those with revenues of $10 million and above) grew online donations by 14.9 percent; medium-sized organization (with revenues of $1 million to $10 million) grew by 9.2 percent; and small organizations (those bringing in under $1 million annually) increased their online revenue streams by 8 percent.

However, while online giving is a growing and driving force within income development for nonprofits, it is only a small part of what fundraising in the future will look like.

---

[1]http://forums.blackbaud.com/blogs/connections/archive/2009/10/01/2009-online-giving-trends-q3.aspx.

As a side note for the fundraisers out there, we are in love with the ever-updated Blackbaud Index of Online Giving. The index is a broad-based fundraising index that reports online revenue trends of more than 1,669 nonprofit organizations representing $424.6 million in yearly revenue on a monthly basis. It is based on actual revenue statistics from nonprofit organizations of all sizes representing arts, culture, and humanities; education; environment and animals; healthcare; human services; international affairs; and public and society benefit sectors. You can read more about it at www.blackbaud.com.

Five Major Changes for the Next Five Years

In order to give you an idea of what we think the big picture of the future of nonprofit fundraising will look like, here are our top five predictions that will most affect the field through 2016 and beyond.

Social Gaming with Rewards

Social gaming refers to the idea that participants earn virtual items for goals they complete in online networks. Some examples of effective use of this technique are the badges you earn in FourSquare, the coins you earn in HelpAttack! or the extra virtual items you earn in the game Farmville on Facebook. In fact, online gaming companies like Zynga (a private company worth more than $5.5 billion and creator of Farmville) already have 350 million users with 65 million daily users as of 2011[2] so—while some of you may see the idea of rewarding donors for their support by sending them a thank you gift as used by nonprofits like PBS—we see the extension of it into the online world as a natural progression; one that is poised to grow when aligned with the interests of today's youth market. We see it as a truly important future path for nonprofit fundraising.

Social gaming and reward-based systems are built using "game theory" to understand and drive constituent interactions. Game theory focuses on creating a user experience that drives the

---

[2]http://www.zynga.com/about/facts.php

consumer to interact with your organization in a way that drives value to both parties. Game theory informs organizations about how to maximize the benefit to their constituents by providing them interesting engagements that hold their attention, entertain them, and ultimately drive organizational mission metrics.[3] To take this further from idea into action, think about the kinds of ways that you thank your supporters for their donations, and think about how you offer incentives to them to increase their donation levels. Traditionally, when you donate at a certain level while participating with the American Cancer Society's Making Strides Against Breast Cancer, you receive a pink sweatshirt. When you donate at the $40 level to your local PBS television station, you receive yet another Ken Burns coffee mug. So why not combine the rewards that are now so popular in online gaming and use them to encourage people to give to your nonprofit? You can do it in a number of different ways.

Jonas Lamis, chief operating officer (COO) and cofounder of Piryx, Inc. (a social fundraising software company) talks about how adding a "game layer" to your connection with donors is technology that will be absolutely pervasive in the next five years:

> "A fundraising event in 2012 features a scavenger hunt with teams competing in real-time, both online and in cities across the globe to collect photos, videos, and donations, with their social networks cheering them on. Elsewhere, a wildlife charity has the number one game on Facebook—"Circle of Life"—where throngs of casual gamers nurture the ecosystem of an African water hole. And yet elsewhere, a shopper at Target "checked-in" to get a share of Target's charity budget to flow to their favorite cause. All three scenarios are examples of the Game Layer."

What Lamis is describing is a completely integrated game where an outside entity, such as Target or Best Buy, is being brought into the fundraising effort because their constituents are being encouraged to seek out those opportunities and find new money. In rewarding your constituents for being creative and finding new revenue

---

[3]http://plato.stanford.edu/entries/game-theory/#Games

streams—and making that praise public—you are creating a second level of competition amongst the constituents outside of the formalized organization; the competition to earn exclusive and unique praise from the organization for extraordinary finds or effort.

An example of how this might look in the future: Susan, a new donor, visits your nonprofit website due to an amazing message she received in her social network's inbox (she received it in her social network's inbox because she only uses email for work). She decides to use her universal pay-phrase, a single sign-in for online financial transactions, in the donation box and donates $40 to help support your cause. Once this is complete, she gets the normal donation thank you screen plus an SMS text message thanking her. This also triggers a social network wall post from your organization to her if she wants to be recognized in public. However, on top of all this, she earns a green heart badge, *and it is this token gift that is the integration of game theory.*

This gift is a virtual item that has a code attached to it, and that code enables the nonprofit that Susan donated to to further engage her in a number of online venues. In theory, it could provide Susan an interactive experience on the nonprofit's website later on (due to the 10-digit code on the badge), or it could tie directly into a social gaming network that Susan is already on. It could also be possible for Susan to unlock a unique branded item on a social networking game site (such as games like Farmville or others that exist in the future). Think of it as a new form of corporate social responsibility—but *fun.* Thus, Susan's donation to your nonprofit not only makes her feel good, it gives her recognition and it also gives her a real-world—yet virtual—prize.

This scenario also ties into the rise of the "social gamer."[4] The rise of the social gamer is very interesting indeed and it's not just people you might consider "geeks" that are playing these online games. A study from the market research firm The NPD Group shows that one out of every five Americans over the age of six has played an online social game at least once.[5] Altogether, that's nearly 60 million Americans, adults and kids alike.

---

[4]http://www.casualconnect.org/content/Seattle/2008/socialcasualsea08.htm
[5]http://www.casualconnect.org/content/Seattle/2008/socialcasualsea08.htm

According to the report, "35 percent of social network gamers are new to gaming, never having participated in any other type of gaming before they started playing games on social networks. Females and older age groups are more likely to be new gamers than other groups measured in the study."

Interesting to us is that despite the perception that social network gamers are primarily females, the study finds that social network gamers are fairly evenly divided between genders with 47 percent of them male, and 53 percent female. This of course goes against the primary stereotype of gamers being males in their teens and twenties.

While you can play most of these social games for free, it is worth noting that 10 percent of social network gamers have spent real money playing these games and 11 percent of them indicate that they are likely to make a future purchase. That's a pretty interesting stat for fundraisers to pay attention to. Anita Frazier, an industry analyst for The NPD Group, hits this point home when we consider the following: "Although 35 percent of social network gamers are new to gaming, it's clear that a lot of existing gamers have been drawn into the social network gaming arena as well. This impacts both the time they spend with other types of gaming as well as the amount of money they're spending on gaming. As more players are drawn into these games, the entire games industry is going to feel, and have to adjust to, the impact."

And according to the folks at Mashable.com, "In 2009, Internet users bought around $2.2 billion worth of virtual goods; experts forecast that number will increase to $6 billion by 2013. And the best-performing social games can inspire repeat purchases in around 41 percent of users. Some stats peg North American gamers' average expenditure per user at $74 over just four months."[6]

For the fundraisers reading this, you can see the potential in the market, especially given that the "female-head-of-household-with-money-to-spend" audience is something you are very used to targeting in your fundraising efforts. In the future, you'll not only have your real-world efforts to target this group, but ever increasingly, you'll need to target this group in the virtual world if you want to

---

[6]http://mashable.com/2010/08/11/social-gaming-business/

survive and thrive. The messages you use to reach them will inevitably change over the next ten years but the audience will be there and they will be listening.

The other advantage of these opportunities is that your non-profit won't have to be heavily invested in the merchandising game and spending donations on real-world items and all the things that go along with it (like worrying about sizes, shipping, etc.). Instead you will be able to concentrate on finding online gaming partners to co-market with, or build your own gaming system to reward donors.

Donating with Ease/The Wet Nap Interface

For a long time we—and a lot of other people—have frowned on many a nonprofit donation form. Not only for the horrible interface, but also in terms of the enormous download times and tons of required fields. Most importantly, though, we frown on the forms because we are tired of nonprofit organizations telling us *how* we can donate. We call the interface of the future the "Wet Nap" interface because it translates an idea of the essence of simplicity: When you enjoy a messy meal, you are given a wet nap. There are no instructions. You open it and use it. Such is the ease of the Wet Nap interface when it comes to design and use.

In 2016 you will see donation forms that present a multitude of payment options. Not just American Express, Discover, Visa, and MasterCard, but PayPal, Google Checkout, Amazon.com account, Rapid Reward points, Social Network gaming currency, frequent flier miles, and more. Jonas Lamis, COO of Piryx, Inc., says, "The world of alternative currencies is about to get very interesting. As more dollars, euros, and yen are converted to 'in-world currencies,' causes will be there to solicit them. Yet for many nonprofits today, account-ing practices are woefully static and manually intensive. For some organizations, it takes three to five people to touch an online donation before a receipt can be issued. Even basic compliance matters, like the proper treatment of donor financial information, can be a tremendous task for these causes."

For these reasons, there's no time like the present to start future casting about how you need to make up the distance between where you are and where you'll need to be. We believe the rise of Internet startup companies will affect alternative currency donations in two ways:

1. The next generation of payment gateways will be created on the Internet, pushing innovations with banks and getting huge clients like Zappos.com to accept the alternative currencies. The consumer will ask, "If I can pay with this currency on Facebook, why can't I use it on Zappos.com, or on my favorite nonprofit site?" As big online businesses pioneer the use of alternative currencies it will eventually become a new and expected part of online commerce. This will of course affect nonprofits and influence how they accept donations.
2. The rise of innovative startups that actually build and *manage* the new donation form of the future. In the same way that a lot of organizations rely on outside companies to manage their online donation processing systems, there is going to be a move to outsource the *development and management* of the actual donation form. Outsourcing this component of the constituent experience will give the nonprofit the ability to constantly adapt and change to the new and preferred types of alternative currencies.

As part of our future casting efforts we also believe you will see the rise of the *payment phrase*, similar to what is currently being developed and deployed on Amazon.com while you are shopping. CNET.com explains Amazon's payphrase system as, "designed to let busy shoppers store their name, address, and payment information in a single phrase and pin code. Instead of entering all that data at the online checkout counter, you type your phrase and pin number when it's time to cough up the cash."[7]

With wide-scale adoption online, alternative currencies will be a new way to pay online instantly. In the near future you won't need to remember your PayPal password or get your purse out to make a payment. All you will need to do is remember your payphrase. It will be fascinating to see if this scales to real-life transactions as well! We can see the credit card swipe machine of today instead just asking two sets of information. We believe by using a unique payment phrase

---

[7]http://news.cnet.com/8301-10797_3-10386056-235.html#ixzz10fgFL9xU

(that ties to your chosen currency and payment type) and verifying two sets of information you will be able to make a donation to your favorite nonprofit seamlessly in 2016. It truly will be that easy.

Part of the beauty of an online transaction is the amount of data that the nonprofit organization gathers from its donors. In the future, nonprofits will still get a robust set of data from their donors' pay-phrase transactions and other online interactions, however, it will only scale up; the amount of information collected on each transaction will be mind blowing. The additional information that the nonprofit could gather from online transactions will transform their ability to target constituents based on geographic and personal information.

Of course the other side of this opportunity will be the need for a way to preserve user privacy online. It will be a tough battle fought by many for-profit and nonprofit businesses. As Jeff Chester, executive director of the Center for Digital Democracy, explains, "Computational advertising enables companies to compile billions of discrete data points and create an analysis of a particular individual and how that person relates with friends, places, geographic infor-mation," so the key will be balancing things as you make donating as easy and functional as possible for your audience. In the future, then, this may be what Susan will see as she donates.

Amount:
Payment Phrase:
Currency Type:
Pin Number:

OR

The name of your first pet:
The name of your high school mascot:

That's it! Of course, people will also have the option to dynami-cally change currency or the biometric questions asked using a simple AJAX interface that dynamically links back to the payment gateway that powers this. So, if you can't remember your PIN num-ber for some reason, you would be able to click the button and instead it will ask you the name of your first pet.

Simplicity is the ultimate form of a great user interface. The technology described here will be flexible to accommodate a wide variety of donation opportunities by creating an overly simplified interface, one in which the nonprofit can ask more questions or fewer. The burden of disclosure, then, will be on the person donating, not the nonprofit. However, nonprofit organizations will need to be very careful about how much information they ask for so as not to put too many barriers in front of the donors.

Again, we see another balance that needs to be struck between your desire for donor information and the desire of the donor to turn that information over. It's a perfect example of game theory, actually: Two parties are trying to maximize their personal gain while trying to engage one another.

And, finally, simple interfaces like the one just described will be perfectly suited for all the mobile devices of 2016 and beyond.

The Rise of the Fun *Local Event/Individual Fundraiser*

Much as we saw the rise of the team fundraising event from the late 1980s into the new millennium, we will start to see its decline as we enter into 2016 and beyond. The proof is in the numbers. According to stats from the RUN. WALK. RIDE. conference of 2010,[8] the top 30 "thon" (i.e., Walk-A-Thon, Bike-A-Thon, Swim-A-Thon) fundraising programs were down from $1.76 billion in 2008. That information was published in the Run Walk Ride Fundraising Council's fourth annual "Run Walk Ride Thirty" study report. The collective $133.9-million drop was the first overall decrease in revenue ever recorded.

In fact we also have seen the world's largest fundraising event, the American Cancer Society's Relay For Life, shrink over the past three years. We credit some of that to the economic recession of 2008 and 2009, however it's also a shift in the way people live and the time they have. The idea of creating a team, recruiting members, sending emails, collecting dues, and attending dozens of planning meetings does not fly with today's 20 and 30 year olds. As they grow and mature, we don't think this will change. What you will see blossom in 2016 and beyond is the rise of individual fundraisers doing fun things, and you will see large nonprofits encouraging people to

---

[8]http://www.runwalkride.com/page.asp?ID=860

do this. It's just not a scalable model to hire hundreds if not thousands of people to manage and run events powered by volunteers.

The challenge comes back to structure. The fundraising model of the future is going to depend on our ability to create and maintain a flexible structure. The trend that we see from our awareness scanning is the individualization of fundraising. In the future, the number of fundraising opportunities will increase and the size of the events will decrease. The driver of this macro trend is that technology is enabling individuals to execute the kind of events that an organization used to have to be involved in to make happen.

Further, free tools and technologies will move into the hands of individuals. In fact, it is already happening. Technology systems such as Donor Drive, a digital fundraising platform that is similar to Blackbaud and Convio products, allow individuals to create and deliver unique special fundraising events. Moving forward, nonprofits will need to think of clever and innovative fundraising concepts, and then let people run with the ideas.

Or, future nonprofits will need to learn to cede control to their volunteers and trust them to come up with their own ideas and execute them outside the formal structure of the organization. It's a scary thought, we know. However, by 2016 people will be ready to take your brand and message and run with it throughout dozens of online and offline networks. People will sign up online, create a page, upload a photo, and start fundraising for their individual causes or passions. The tools will empower them, and so it is up to you to begin to understand the untapped potential in this version of the fundraising future state.

Thon Morse, CEO of online fundraising company KIMBIA, says "Most online fundraising tools still rely on the concept of direct response, which treats the donor as a consumer. On the Web, however, donors can not only give, but they can also share and create." He goes on to say, "The future of fundraising, thus, will not depend on a successful response to a single mass email message that has been *personalized* but instead, it will be propelled by the use of truly *personal* messages—direct and diverse appeals that create a cascade of response and donor engagement." In addition, the idea of raising funds online is not new but the idea of forming teams (outside of the corporate workplace and legacy teams) will be an antique fundraising tactic. We are already seeing the rise of this in a couple of ways.

Movember. In 2009, a grassroots awareness and fundraising event known as Movember raised more than $19,000,000, with more than 2,000 people registered to support the Movember Foundation, a nonprofit dedicated to fighting prostate cancer and raising male cancer awareness.[9]

The success of the Movember campaign is based on the fact that the Movember foundation engages individuals in fundraising in their own creative and unique ways, and not having a "command and conquer" system with prescribed fundraising methodologies, rules, and regulations. They let potential fundraisers join teams if they want to, but don't pressure them. They then let them fundraise for an exact time period and they make it *fun*.

You see, Movember is all about raising awareness and funds for men's cancer issues. They do this by encouraging men to show off their ability to grow and customize their mustaches (Figure 9.1). Not only do Movember men and women (known as Bros and Mos) raise funds, but the men actually do something physical. Movember requires men to make a physical investment in growing a mustache and, in doing so, the men have a sense of commitment not only to the Movember organization but also to the other men participating. Through this joint physical activity Movember is creating a very strong bond between men and their Bros. Movember doesn't involve t-shirt sizes or dozens of team captain meetings. It involves growing facial hair. And of course when people ask the men why they are growing their mustaches, they have an advertising opportunity. Also, Movember men get the opportunity to advocate for their cause for a whole month! Not one weekend, but a full 30 days, And since the month of Movember takes place every November worldwide, all of the Movember Bros are talking about the issues simultaneously, amplifying the volume of the message.

Even more impressive is that the only overhead that Movember has at the end of the month is to throw a giant costume/gala party where the costume matches the mustache. And, of course, this is a cleverly disguised donor/fundraising thank-you party.

Strut Your Mutt. Best Friends Animal Society, a nationwide animal rescue group, launched Strut Your Mutt, a new annual dog walk

---

[9]http://www.givewell.com.au/details_name.asp?txtOrganisation=NOV

Figure 9.1   David's Movember Moustache

and festival in Los Angeles and New York, which raised more than $340,000 for Best Friends community programs in those cities and participating local animal rescue/welfare groups, with $207,000 going directly to the groups.

Best Friends opened this fundraising opportunity to their local Network Charities, all 501(c)3 organizations that are working toward achieving a world of No More Homeless Pets. Almost 40 of Best Friends' Network Charities participated in Strut Your Mutt by forming walk teams, or "dog packs," and rallying their supporters to join their packs and fundraise for them. The charities were given all of the money that their packs raised (minus credit card transaction fees), including registration fees; the top packs raised almost $30,000.

While a run/walk event is not new or unique to fundraising, Best Friends Strut Your Mutt is an innovative fundraising model because it used the cause, not the organization, as the platform for raising money, and allowed an opportunity for multiple organizations with similar missions to raise money in the same space by engaging and inspiring their own supporters.

Because Best Friends covered the costs for hosting Strut Your Mutt, smaller groups without the budgets to pay marketing and production costs associated with large-scale events were able to piggyback on Strut Your Mutt and use it as their fall fundraising initiatives.

Glimmer of Hope. The nonprofit Glimmer of Hope has a simple mission. End the world's water problems. Not too shabby, huh? When we talked to Marianne Lind, Director of Marketing at

Glimmer of Hope, about their mission, she said: "With Glimmer's new online fundraising platform we wanted more than just a way to make giving fun. We focused on designing a system that would inspire passion in users. What does it mean to give in a way that doesn't leave the giver feeling hollow? A Glimmer of Hope created a model that allows people to give in a meaningful way. When we set out to design this new system, we kept that in mind."

In 2009, a community of companies led by an Austin firm called Projekt 202, collaborated pro-bono with A Glimmer of Hope to create a next-generation fundraising platform to help lift rural villages in Africa out of extreme poverty. The system allows users to build their own personal mission statement by making choices that include: what region of the country do you want to work in and what type of project do you want 100 percent of your donations to fund (a water well, school, health clinic, or microfinance loan).

This new, Drupal-based platform allows users to create compelling personal campaigns based on what inspires them, and share their inspirations with others. Users can customize their own videos, import their contacts, post their campaign to social media accounts, blog about their e-philanthropy journey, and earn journal and passport-like badges for their personal and group achievements.

Projekt 202 combines successful principles from gaming sites, good UX design with the effective use of rich media to help build trust and credibility online. This new system makes online giving fun and motivates participants to keep coming back, which builds a sense of community. This is key in 2016 and beyond.

■ ■ ■

All three of the examples in the previous section are great fundraising case studies that rely on the long tail of fundraising to happen.

The Socially Conscious Partnership

In the early 2000s, we saw the rise of corporate social responsibility (CSR) in for-profit companies. In fact, some larger companies now have a social responsibility officer with an actual department. This stems from the idea that for-profit organizations should be engaging and giving back to their local communities, the environment, and to social causes. CSR has been enacted on the local community level and all the way up to the global stage.

In most cases a CSR engagement takes shape in one of two main ways: A large-scale donation/grant/scholarship program, or actually branding products with a nonprofit angle. You can see this in 2011 with the partnerships between the American Heart Association and General Mills foods or the branding of Susan G. Komen and Yoplait yogurt.

As CSR activity grows, some people are skeptical of the true impact that their branded-product purchase is having on the actual mission of the various causes. The idea is that nonprofits are straying a little too far away from their missions and for-profit organizations are taking advantage of the nonprofit logos to sell all kinds of products. Even as early as 2008, a *Time* article talks about "Pink-Washing" and describes it as an overwhelming co-option of the Pink Ribbon on products. In most cases, the Pink Ribbon denotes that proceeds of a sale are bound for a worthy cause, but in a world with so many organizations and so many causes, the volume of CSR-branded products can become overwhelming.[10]

The examples of this are almost laughable when thinking about the pink ribbon to denote breast cancer awareness. The pink ribbon is on everything and there are tons of products that have been turned pink, from DVD players to cans of soup. When do advertising opportunities start to take away from both the nonprofit and for-profit brands? And how much do these campaigns actually raise?

Unfortunately this is not something that will stop by 2016. If anything, we predict it will dramatically increase. As long as nonprofits can avoid the ire of the unrelated business income tax (UBIT) from the IRS, they will push the limits of what they sell and who they partner with for sales and advertising. With that said, by 2016 and beyond we will see a rise in actually viable for-profit and nonprofit partnerships in the form of businesses that have a double bottom line of profits and doing good. A few businesses that exist as of the writing of this book are HelpAttack!, GivShop, GOOD, KIIMBY, and Supportland.

These businesses were not founded just to turn a profit from nonprofits. They were founded to solve an issue in the marketplace while helping nonprofits. They do this in a variety of ways, all the

---

[10]http://www.time.com/time/connections/article/0,9171,1543947,00.html

while working hand in hand with nonprofits to help generate donations, raise awareness of their mission, and advertise their services. Here is how they work.

HelpAttack!. HelpAttack! is an online fundraising company. And their product is a fun and easy way for you to turn social actions into social good. Starting with Twitter in 2010 and Facebook soon after, HelpAttack! allows you to pledge an amount of money for each action you take in a social network, and then give it to your favorite nonprofits. All the while you are unlocking coins, discovering new nonprofits and causes you might like to support, and helping do everything from plant trees to feed the homeless.

HelpAttack! leverages the game theory (through the coins you earn) we previously talked about to create an engaging experience for its users. By creating a competitive environment, HelpAttack! delivers an addictive experience that delivers tangible support for social causes. The simplicity and effortless interface is the future of nonprofit engagement. Capitalizing on everyday actions to drive results is an emerging aspect that you will definitely see in many future nonprofit organization engagement campaigns.

GivShop. GivShop is a website located at Givshop.com and it works similarly to Groupon. People sign up to receive daily emails with a deeply discounted deal from a local Austin, Texas, business. Similar to the Groupon model, a certain number of people have to purchase the deal for it to take effect. This guarantees the business will be able to turn a profit on the deal. However, unlike Groupon, the folks at GivShop give 50 percent of their profit to local charities, then users select a nonprofit from the list and they receive a part of the deal. Their motto is that "group buying becomes group giving!"[11] In this way, GivShop is a socially responsible business that not only makes a living off consumers, but also channels funds back toward development of local nonprofits.

GivShop.com is an exceptionally powerful model because it leverages a naturally occurring behavior—shopping—and channels that behavioral action into a mutually beneficial outcome for all parties involved. The magic of the GivShop.com model is that it

---

[11]http://www.givshop.com/austin/how-it-works

allows the donor to select the receiving organization. Therefore donors who have a particular affinity for a charity have a higher likelihood of using this system since their actions can directly impact their charity of choice.

GOOD. *GOOD* magazine is another example of an organization that allows its buyers to route their donations to a charity of their choice. *GOOD* continues to publish quarterly magazines, run a very compelling website (www.good.is), and deliver daily Good alerts to its subscribers, while donating hundreds of thousands of dollars to worthy causes around the world—in an environment when *Newsweek* magazine sold for $1.[12]

KIIMBY. KIIMBY—started in Austin, Texas, in 2010—stands for keep it in my backyard and can be found at KIIMBY.com. KIIMBY donors present a KIIMBY card to retailers and their transaction earns shoppers KIIMBY points that can be redeemed for access to exclusive community events, activities, and offers. The best way to think about the KIIMBY card is as a high-powered community loyalty card that makes it easy and fun to discover and show your support for local businesses and nonprofits.[13]

When you use your KIIMBY card while shopping at a member business, that shop takes a small percentage of the sale and directs it to the nonprofits that shoppers have selected in their KIIMBY member profiles. Thus generating micro-donations to the nonprofits in the Austin community. In talking with local Austin nonprofits the most exciting thing for them is that they will have comprehensive analytics from the card on who supports them and what businesses drive the most donations…Something they never had data on before. Once again we see a socially responsible business that has a double bottom line.

SUPPORTLAND. The city of Portland, Oregon, has a similar program that is encouraging shoppers to engage and patronize

---

[12]http://www.huffingtonpost.com/2010/08/02/sidney-harman-newsweek-pu_n_667448.html
[13]http://www.kiimby.com/faq

local businesses, called Supportland.[14] Supportland is a rewards program that gives users points for their patronage, and those points are redeemable at other participating retailers. Buy a grill from a local hardware store and earn 50 points. Use 40 of those points for a hamburger from a local butcher shop and enjoy. The fundraising of the future will more actively engage the local economy on the micro scale and strive to make large-scale causes local. By intertwining local commerce with the locally organized fundraiser you create a supportive base for future events and interaction.

The Shift in Donor Attitudes

If you look at the shift in fundraising over time from door-to-door to the phone, mail, email, the Web, and social media sites, you will also be able to see a fundamental shift in donors' attitudes. We think this will be a huge change from now through 2016 and beyond, and want you be ready for it.

According to a study of 8,000 Americans and 7,000 Canadians of all ages and giving levels (as well as 42 American and Canadian nonprofits) done by the firm Cygnus Applied Research, there is a "definite shift in giving, paving the way for a new, independent donor." "They do their research online and make confident choices," says Penelope Burk, president of Cygnus Applied Research. "Fundraising needs to adapt to this proactive donor who won't be told when and how to give."[15]

Some other prominent shifts uncovered in this attitude study were that three out of four donors said they could be inspired to give even more to charitable causes this year, although young and middle-aged donors have a growing preference for supporting fewer nonprofits. Also, according to survey respondents, nonprofits could raise more money by asking less often. More than 70 percent of donors say they now drop charities or give less than they could to those that over-solicit.

The survey also backed up the independent, confident donor by saying that nearly 75 percent of respondents are more likely to favor

---

[14]http://supportland.com/
[15]http://www.cygresearch.com/press/pressrelease-CDS-2010.php

giving to nonprofits that provide them with "measurable results on what has been or is being achieved with donors' contributions."

According to Penelope Burk at Cygnus, failure to receive measurable return on investment (ROI) on their donations remains the number one reason donors stop giving or give less than they could. "Nothing is more important than getting this right," she notes. "It's the key that unlocks the door to sustainable fundraising, regardless of the economy."

Peter Frumkin, Ph.D., at the RGK center for Philanthropy and Community Service, says in his book *The Essence of Strategic Giving* [16] that there are five psychological choices that donors make before they give. The four we found interesting (and think apply even to small donors) are:

1. Declaring the public value to be produced through their private giving.
2. Recognizing how a donation fits with a donor's own identity and style.
3. Being aware of the time frame that guides a gift.
4. Specifying the intended impact being pursued.

As you read this list, think about the following: When is the last time you thought of donations to your organization through these lenses? This is how the modern donor gives and these key factors will only intensify in the future as donors learn more and more from multiple data points about your nonprofit. You only have to use your imagination to think of all the ways the donor of the future will have oversight into how your nonprofit does business. Woe to the nontransparent organization of 2016!

A Word about Transparency in Nonprofits of the Future

Since donors will be more educated, proactive, and scarce in the future, how do you rate and judge the transparency of your nonprofit now and in the future? Most nonprofits will probably respond, "Not very well."

---

[16]http://www.press.uchicago.edu/presssite/metadata.epl?mode=synopsis& bookkey=9009275

When you break it down, there are a small handful of watchdog organizations scrutinizing nonprofits, including Charity Navigator, Guide Star and the Better Business Bureau. In 2010, a British research and consulting firm, YouGov, released the results of a study on whether donors are interested in charity ratings. The report was headlined, "Mixed response toward grading system for charities."[17]

According to the survey, 68 percent of people would switch their donations to another charity if they found the one they were supporting was performing badly. So far, that makes sense. But only 40 percent—a substantial minority, but still a minority—are interested in a charity rating system to provide independent assessments of organizations.

Martin Brooks of New Philanthropy Capital's blog writes, "Given this, it is hardly surprising to find that 68 percent of people think that an independent rating system would not affect their giving decisions . . . There is something strange in these figures. In particular, the fact that 68 percent say they would change the pattern of donations if they were given evidence of poor performance, and the same percentage saying they would not respond to independent evidence. Reconciling these is tricky."[18]

Do we not trust our own giving decisions? Who are we to say that any of these online watchdogs are really doing their job, anyway? Ask yourself some critical questions. How are these sites supported? Is it ad revenue? Donations? Who runs them? Do nonprofits pay to be included? Are anonymous reviews allowed? Can nonprofits respond to comments à la Yelp.com? Charity rating systems also have to contain a level of transparency that the assessments in the reviews they give are honest, in good faith, and are intended to inform the public in an unbiased manner.

We think there will be a lot more of these sites as we move toward 2016 and beyond, but donors will consult and rely on them less and less. Why? As we mentioned, donors will have hundreds of datapoints to check up on their preferred nonprofit in the future. Soon you will be judged not only on the marketing and advertising

---

[17]http://newphilanthropycapital.wordpress.com/2010/06/02/do-enough-donors-care/
[18]http://newphilanthropycapital.wordpress.com/2010/06/02/do-enough-donors-care/

that you produce but by the information they find on you in a basic Google search: Everything from what your social media site's responses look like to what donation currencies your accept to your past year's annual video report on YouTube. Your public presence will dramatically affect donor perceptions and donor attitudes.

Besides the many ideas and examples we have given you here, there are some other really excellent resources available if you want to understand even more about what donor behavior will look like in 2016 and beyond. We encourage you to read *Nudge* by Richard H. Thaler and Cass R. Sunstein, and *Blink* by Malcom Gladwell. Both of these books examine the psychology behind why people make the decisions they make. Neither book is written specifically for nonprofit fundraisers but they each provide amazing insight into why people do what they do, and these findings easily extrapolate to the type of giving and fundraising decisions we are discussing here.

Example from the Front Lines: Alan Graham of Mobile Loaves and Fishes, and Kate Donaho of T3

For a couple of years now, David has been volunteering and working with Mobile Loaves and Fishes, a nationwide homeless advocacy nonprofit based in Austin, Texas. David began as a volunteer blogging about the work they do and moved into raising funds, participating in a street retreat (which he videotaped), and consulting on social media. He also helped organize Social Media Club Austin to raise more than $2,000 for Mobile Loaves and Fishes. This exposure from the power of fundraising via social media led to the case study and fundraising campaign described in this article by Kate Donaho of T3. At T3, Kate is the group creative director and contributing thinker. This article appeared on the Advertising Age *GoodWorks blog on June 2, 2010.*

A few weeks ago, we put a homeless person on a billboard. Not a striking photograph of a homeless person, or a clever headline about homelessness, but an actual homeless man named Danny Silver. This was part of a campaign to raise money and awareness for our client, Mobile Loaves and Fishes (MLF), an Austin-based mission that serves food and clothing to the homeless and working poor.

The result was a truly *positive ROI*: Within 48 hours, we raised enough money to get Danny and his wheelchair-bound wife off the streets and into a home, as well as funds for MLF and national awareness of the issue. We also learned a few priceless lessons about the intersection of mobile and social media, traditional advertising and effective PR.

How It Happened

The project started when our agency, T3, helped to set up a text-message donation platform for MLF. After that, several of us became volunteers, going out on monthly catering truck runs to deliver food. We knew we could do more, so we signed on as MLF's pro-bono agency.

From our perspective, the biggest challenge to getting someone to help a homeless person was first getting them to *see* a homeless person. We wanted to raise the cloak of invisibility that makes people look away rather than help.

Our core campaign idea was born: "I Am Here." (See Figure 9.2.) Our goal was to create a campaign that would not only launch the text-to-give option, but also raise awareness about the organization's mission. We knew "I Am Here" would have creative components across all media. But we needed to kick it off with something that would say "I am here" in a way that no one could ignore. Something like... well... putting a homeless guy up on a billboard. We said it enough times that it started to sound like a legitimate idea. We decided to keep pursuing it until someone said no. Nobody did.

And that's how, April 27 and 28, Danny, along with MLF founder Alan Graham, wound up at the top of a billboard on I-35.

Figure 9.2   I Am Here
Source: T3, www.t-3.com.

What We Learned

Assume it *can* be done. How many ideas have been killed by comments like, "we could never pull that off" or "there's no way the client will approve it" before they ever went anywhere? Some great ones, sadly. Our idea got off the ground, literally, because we were optimistic, persistent, and lucky enough to have a courageous client like Alan at MLF and a bold partner like Reagan Outdoor, who donated the billboard space. (A little bravado, some harness rope, and a few legal waivers didn't hurt either!)

Find a story to tell. The billboard event provided a platform to tell a story: The chronicle of Danny and Maggie's lives and the new home and beginning that were imminent. As that story unfolded, people tuned in around Austin, and across the country. In fact, one of the people watching was Danny's daughter, whom he hadn't seen in 10 years. She reached out to Alan after seeing the news coverage, and he flew her to Austin to reunite with Danny on move-in day, creating quite a happy ending, indeed.

All channels work harder, together. It was the combination of media that made our campaign a success: The live event featured in a traditional medium, with the immediacy of a mobile call-to-action, supported by video storytelling, distributed via social media and good old-fashioned public relations. In 48 hours, we raised the $12,000 we needed through texting. In eight days, we got more than 1.3 million impressions on Twitter and Facebook.

Buzz doesn't always translate to dollars. People were going crazy tweeting and retweeting, spreading the word to help Danny, but of those 20,000 people, less than 2 percent texted donations. We were shocked: People were impassioned, but they weren't doing what we needed them to do: text. It turns out that most people wanted to donate online, because that's where they were. The online donations were significant, and they continue to roll in.

PR is a gamble, but it can pay off big. We had no media budget, so we had to rely on public relations to give us the reach we wanted. Essentially, we had to bet on the story we were telling, and our crafty PR team got on the phone telling it. We got lucky, with coverage everywhere from CNN to the *Huffington Post*. To date, "I Am Here" has been covered on 230 news outlets in 30 markets, and the media value of the news coverage is more than half a million dollars.

Have the social conversations—even the fierce ones. We knew we'd stir controversy, and while the vast majority of feedback was positive, we had to welcome the negative as well. Alan, already an avid user of social media, spent most of his time that week, when not twittering or live streaming from the billboard, answering tough questions and responding to concerns. His willingness to have an authentic, passionate dialogue greatly advanced his cause.

The soft metrics matter. Alan says that his mission is to change the world one human at a time. By extension, the goal of "I Am Here" was to change one heart at a time. The stories continue to trickle in: Just yesterday a friend of mine met a Canadian guy in a bar in California. When the friend said he was from Austin, the Canadian said, "Huh. Is that homeless guy still up on a billboard?" My friend said no, the guy was down now, but explained that he knew the organization and the people that worked on the campaign. The man responded, "Well, tell them they did good."

Conclusion

Kate Donaho's article shows us that there is a greater need than ever before to make a strong personal connection in order to raise funds from donors. Regardless of the channel that we use, the basic concept remains the same: We have to make our causes resonate with donors if we expect them to support us. The Web just so happens to be a growing and vibrant change in the channel.

It is common sense that the future of fundraising will be on the Web. It can't be changed or denied. Nonprofits that are spending thousands of dollars on direct mail and major gifts brochures as their primary avenue for recruiting donors and retaining funds will soon go the way of the Bali Tiger. Failure to adapt to the new environmental realities has one predictable result: extinction.

The true future of fundraising on the Web remains an elusive mix. What is definitive, though, is the importance of knowing your constituents, asking for funds at the right time, and making it as fun and easy as possible for them to donate and share their donation experience with others. The nonprofit that masters this by 2016 will certainly position themselves for success in the future.

Next up, in Chapter 10, we lay out the most critical trends we see in nonprofit communication over the next five years.

CHAPTER 10

The Future of Communications

*Moving forward, fundraisers will need to become more sophisticated
in combining both traditional channels and new media while also
investing in the proper tools and resources to ensure all fundraising
programs are truly integrated and meet the ever-changing
communication preferences of donors.*

— Lisa Goddard, Capitol Area Food Bank

Good future casting involves getting involved in awareness exercises and forming an educated guess as to what is going to happen next. Future casts are almost always based on extrapolating current trends and mixing them with creative thinking to see what the different possible future scenarios are.

For instance, look around you today and consider what the cell phone is capable of. Now think back to the year 2000 and imagine the cell phone you had back then and think about if you had been able to imagine the possibilities of having a networked computer in the palm of your hand instead. That is the essence of futuring: Recognizing a rising trend and imagining the possibilities that it could produce.

With that as food for your thought, we have created future scans of communication based on experience, insight, and creativity. We know most nonprofits barely do two-year strategic plans much less further down the line so looking 10 years into the future might not be the best place to start. While the ideas and possibilities may be inspirational from that type of exercise, we want to help keep you focused on actionable change that is coming your way more immediately. Let's take a look, then, into the future of communications in our field, starting with the next five years (through the year 2016).

Awareness scanning techniques are not just for product innovation programs but can also provide valuable insights during any long-term strategy planning session for your nonprofit. The best way we have found for nonprofits to stay on top of futuring in their planning is not only by hiring smart staff and recruiting innovative board members, but also by observing and monitoring future trends. And the most valuable part of this exercise is the sharing of information. However you decide to structure your engagement, make sure you make a concerted effort to share documentation with the members of your whole team through a platform like Google Docs, BaseCamp, an internal wiki, or simply sharing emails in a group setting.

Emerging Trends through 2016 and Beyond

In the field of communication we see several trends emerging now that will only get bigger as we move closer to 2016. The five we will present to you here involve Geolocation, Monitoring Communications, Micro Segmentation, Advertising, and Loss of Privacy. As we discuss these trends, think large about the trend itself and try not to focus too intently on the technologies, systems, and vendors we talk about as examples.

A Quick Aside: What?! No Social Media?!

Many people claiming to be "social media experts" may gasp while reading a section on communications without social media being one of the top five emerging trends through 2016. But we believe that by the time 2016 rolls around, social media will just be another everyday part of how you accomplish any of your communications goals. The drive to have a Twitter account, a Facebook account, and a YouTube channel will be a natural part of setting up any campaign for your nonprofit; just as natural as setting up a website for a new program is today. Even as of 2011, social media is more and more of a buzzword used to sell all sorts of products to nonprofits. In fact you could also say that social media today is quickly becoming a way to sell all sorts of "snake oil"-esque products. (One of our favorite examples of this is from the 1920's: "curative electricity."[1])

With this in mind, then, we are going to skip social media in this chapter. There are a ton of books already written on this subject in relation to communications, and even a hundred more blogs that deal with the subject. If you feel you need to read up specifically on it, feel free to check out: *The Networked Nonprofit* by Beth Kanter and Allison Fine, *Social Media 101: Tactics and Tips to Develop Your Business Online* by Chris Brogan, or *Born Digital* by John Palfry and Urs Gasser to learn about the new constituents and how they use the web. You can also check out *Engage: The Complete Guide for Brands and Businesses to Build, Cultivate, and Measure Success in the New Web* by Brian Solis. But remember, social media is not the future. It is now just another part of any marketing/communication campaign.

The Top Five

After evaluating the current digital marketing landscape we chose five overarching trends that we think will persist over the course of the next five years and drive value to your organization. We see longevity in the supporting technology of these trends and the potential for expanding the applications that leverage the trends. We believe these top five will definitely persist over the medium term and could have major impacts on your organization's implementation of digital marketing programs well into the future.

Trend #1: Geolocation: Don't Find Us—We'll Find You!

Although just rising in popularity toward the end of 2009 and into 2010, geolocation will hit its stride in 2012 and continue to grow. The driving factor behind the adoption of geolocation is the GPS-enabled smartphone. You have to have both the service and the phone to deliver a complex geolocation user experience. The GPS lets the phone know where it is, and the smartphone allows the application to interact seamlessly with the home network. Every new smartphone sale is a new potential geolocation system user.

---

[1]http://blog.modernmechanix.com/mags/PhysicalCulture/3-1922/sugar_coated_electricity.jpg

In 2010, there are even some location-based players experimenting with passive background check-ins.[2]

More and more people in the world are using geolocation technology for a variety of reasons. They use it to leave personal tips and advice about a particular location they want others to know about (try the baked ziti at X restaurant—skip the meatballs), to invite their friends to locations, to broadcast meetings they are attending, and to earn rewards for "checking in." Another great feature of a service like Foursquare is that, because it is user-generated and digital, it is almost always current. Never again will you go to a phone book to call and see if a restaurant is still at that location. By the time you read this paragraph most locations in the United States will have some data about them mapped into Foursquare, Gowalla, SCVNGR, or another mobile geolocation system.

Geolocation applications work by allowing the user to download an app to their mobile device or access a mobile website. Once they sign up for an account they have the ability to find their specific location on the service and hit the check-in button. Then, depending on the service, the system checks the GPS to determine if they are really there. If so, they are awarded points that drive a leaderboard/points-type system along with badges and other virtual items. If the location is not present, the user can create it and gain extra points for being the first person to locate and identify it. Users are given the option to share their location with their friends on the service, Twitter, Facebook, or all three. They can also post photos of the location and post a message as they check in.

Need more proof that geolocation is here to stay? Facebook added a check-in/geolocation called "Places" in 2010 and opened the geolocation movement to its then-500-million-person audience.

You can use geolocating services to raise money from merchants. You can also use them to help donors invite friends to events that are taking place, use mobile devices, and to quickly activate a volunteer response to a mission emergency. If you are looking for inspiration, visit the Mobile Active site http://mobileactive.org to learn about a host of other creative ways that nonprofit-organization (NPO) professionals are using mobile and geolocation to drive mission.

---

[2]http://techcrunch.com/2010/06/21/loopt-background-location-iphone/

(We encourage you to visit us on Facebook, too, and list your own ideas on how to use geolocation on our page under Discussions.)

At Lights. Camera. Help. we took the opportunity to create new locations on Foursquare within event locations we were already at. Say for instance we were renting a space called "The Goodlife" in Austin, Texas. We would create our own location on top of it. Then, as we took the stage at the event, we would encourage people to check in at our location by searching for it. Once people checked in, they could also post the info to their social networks and spread the brand awareness of our nonprofit, while at the same time they let their friends know where they were in case they wanted to join them. This increased the attendance at our event in real time.

Danielle Brigida of the National Wildlife Foundation, hit this point home when she said, "Right now my innovative projects revolve around location-based sites like Foursquare and Gowalla. I think there is real potential there to measure how many people are going outside and finding exciting ways to encourage them to check in in parks and nature." She goes on to say, "The excitement of checking in made me think about the connection that we have to a database of ours called Naturefind. I would love to integrate that data so that anytime anyone checks into any of the places on Naturefind we are notified. For now, we just have a page on Foursquare but I'd love to make it so nature is as encouraging as a bar to check into!"

The TEDxCincinnati conference also used the Foursquare service during a conference. In much the same way that Lights. Camera. Help. implemented their strategy, TEDxCincinnati created a new venue within the system especially for the special event. In addition, the organizers encouraged the participants to check in on their preferred geolocation service and look for friends that were in the audience that they may not have known were attending.

The following touches on a few companies (besides Facebook and Foursquare) that will be integral for your NPO to watch through 2016. But first let's look at the service that started all of this.

Dodgeball. Does anyone else remember the mobile application Dodgeball? We know we do! It was founded in 2000, and we both used it to obsessively track each other and danah boyd[3] (whom we suggested you follow in Chapter 5), a preeminent researcher and expert on young people's use of social media, at South by Southwest (SXSW) in 2006. Dodgeball was one of the first-ever geolocation services that let you broadcast your location to other people via text message. Users had to manually text in the name of their location to a central server that would then alert friends that were within a 10-block radius. How old fashioned!

Dodgeball—a great tool for seeing where and what your friends were doing—was created during the heady Internet days of 2000, so privacy was not on the minds of users as we wandered the streets of Austin, Texas. One of the founders of Dodgeball was Dennis Crowley who, after selling the app to Google,[4] quit Google, and went on to cocreate Foursquare with Naveen Selvadurai.[5] The Foursquare service uses GPS data, a mobile phone, and a massive database to enable users to check into venues and earn points and recognition just for saying that they are present. Individuals connect with friends and share their locations, leave tips about local businesses, earn virtual merit badges, and in some cases earn discounts for being a Foursquare user.

Having talked briefly to Crowley at SXSW, we really admire the innovation it took to launch a service such as Dodgeball at such an early time for phones, GPS, and the Web 2.0 movement. Imagine in 2011 having to text your location (spelled correctly) to any of the geolocation services and having it text you back! And, on top of that, imagine being bought by Google and then quitting because they were not providing sufficient support for your project? And then imagine going to start a new venture? Wow. As we said, Dennis never quite gave up on geolocation and went on to bring us the massive hit Foursquare. As of June 2010, Foursquare was adding more than 100,000 new users per week.[6] It is quite the story on perseverance and innovation, no?

---

[3]danah boyd is a social media researcher at Microsoft Research New England and a Fellow at Harvard University's Berkman Center for Internet and Society. www .danah.org
[4]http://valleywag.gawker.com/tech/dodgeball/dodgeball-finally-adopted-google-knows-where-you-drank-last-night-208500.php
[5]www.foursquare.com
[6]http://techcrunch.com/2010/06/22/foursquare-growth/

SCVNGR. SCVNGR is a location-based gaming platform for mobile phones. Besides not being able to afford vowels, they are looking to do something different with their geolocation system. Not only do they want you to check in, they want you to challenge other users. According to the *New York Times*, "The company hopes to entice mobile phone users to create their own games for friends or businesses... You visit a place—say, your favorite burrito shop—open up the Scvngr app and are shown a list of challenges. One challenge might ask you to snap a pic for a couple points. Another to solve some location-based riddle that the owners of the shop have added. And yet a third to do the 'Tin-Foil Origami' challenge where you must carefully unwrap your burrito and create an origami sculpture out of the foil. Snap a photo of your creation for three points!"[7]

Businesses and nonprofits that use this kind of an approach not only create a fun diversion, but they also create a multi-sensory experience for their patrons that depends on the connection between the consumer and the organization.

Gowalla. From deep in the heart of Texas comes this geolocation application with amazing graphics and a deep system of trips for users to experience. The more trips you complete, the more items you can earn. Gowalla recently launched a partnership with Chevy and created a series of trips based around the Texas state fair.

In the future, services like Gowalla will curate experiences, almost like a museum docent. The system allows individuals to create their own trips for others to follow, or Gowalla can create the trip for a sponsor or special event. Trips have information on things to see, places to visit, and activities to do. Chevy set up a series of trips based on unique fair experiences. They include a music-themed "Chevy Rocks" trip, a "Chevy Classic Fair" trip, and of course the "Fried Food Challenge" trip. Each one was designed to help users have a great time (or maybe a belly ache!).

Trend #2: Monitoring Technology—The Rise of #Hashtags

A hashtag, as defined by Twitter, was created because Twitter provided no easy way to group tweets or add extra data. Since Twitter did

---

[7]http://bits.blogs.nytimes.com/2010/05/13/a-new-entry-into-the-world-of-location-based-games/

not develop this capability into its system, the community that used Twitter came up with their own way and the hashtag was born.

A hashtag is similar to other Web tags: it is metadata that helps add tweets to a category. Hashtags have the "hash" or "pound" symbol (#) preceding the tag: #traffic, #followfriday, #hashtag, #movember, #thefutureofnpos, and so on.[8] Just as you might tag a Web bookmark in a social bookmarking site such as Xmarks.com, Del.icio.us, or on your favorite blog platform, in the future the hashtag will be ubiquitous across all social platforms. You will be able to tag everything from Facebook updates to text messages you send your friends. The hashtag could become the universal way to add metadata to a piece of online content.

Public versus Private. We think two important things will rise from the use of hashtags. By using a hashtag on your information, you are able to search for that information across multiple public data streams and see what people are talking about. This will be amazing when you want to learn about the 2017 World Cup (#worldcup). If everyone is using the same hashtag, all the data gets grouped together, which makes it easier to follow the whole global conversation (even the parts you are not actively participating in). This method of using hashtags puts a lot of control into the users' hands because if there is a post they want to make about a topic, but do not want it included in the global conversation, they can decide to just not include a hashtag. If they don't include one, the content is not a part of the public stream search.

Everything Traceable. With the use of hashtags, then, imagine the ROI you could present to a sponsor or major donor about how many times people talked about an event online and across streams. It would be a major win for nonprofits seeking funding and sponsorships for their missions. Imagine if you could see and understand the concerns of your constituents as they express them. This kind of monitoring would deliver real-time intelligence about honest conversations taking place unmediated all over the Web. Then, what you decide to do with that information is up to you. A great

---

[8]http://support.twitter.com/entries/49309-what-are-hashtags-symbols)

example of this is the contest over at http://beatcancereverywhere
.com/, which tracks the hashtag #beatcancer.

Social media has an added benefit of being extremely trackable
and monitorable if you plan ahead. This can be as simple as using
a hashtag when you tweet. When we attended the Texas Nonprofit
Summit in 2010 the hashtag was #TXNS. They announced it on
stage and on Twitter and in the program event, then the crowd,
like the good sheep we are, added this to all our tweets. (We'll talk
more about this in Trend #5 to come.)

Then using the service The Archivist (which is free), the conference organizers were able to send out a graph like the one shown
in Figure 10.1 to all their fans, users, and influencers as well as their
board and sponsors.

At TEDxCincinnati, the hashtag for the event was #TEDxcincy.
We organized the social media for the event so we were able to take
the process one step further. We created a unique hashtag for each
presenter and published it in the conference program. We encouraged all of the audience members and participants to use the hashtags
to help curate the conversations. The added benefit was that during
the conference participants could conduct silent conversations

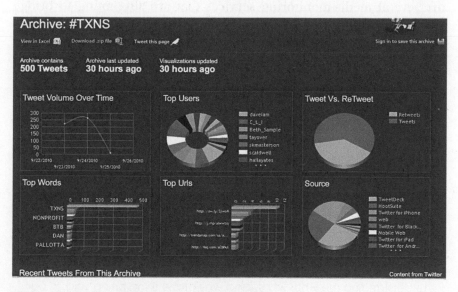

Figure 10.1   The Texas Nonprofit Summit
Source: http://archivist.visitmix.com/ac2e1bdb/1

about the presentations in real time and the hashtags kept the conversations separate. In addition, after the event was over, anyone could use the hashtag to research the conversation days, weeks, and even months later.

James Young, of the social media campaign company Social Agency, told us, "I think the future will bring vast improvements to the algorithms detecting the true sentiment of a message so that our computers will also recognize the nuances of speech that our brains can pick up." He went on to say, "I think the consolidation of our online personas will be complete so that we can easily access a fully fleshed-out biography of the person behind the content."

Some of the Tools Helping to Collect the Information. When imagining a communications department of the future, many of us might envision something out of a science fiction novel; sitting in front of some sort of minority report-type screen that is able to monitor and track every mention of a nonprofit across all forms of media. Will this actually be the case? We think not. However, there is going to be tremendous opportunity for a company that concentrates specifically on nonprofits to innovate and make a huge impact. Right now there are several media-monitoring services that are attempting to bridge the divide between what we can track online versus what we can track through traditional *broadcast* channels. Remember the word *broadcast*? It's from that good old medium of TV, which will still be reaching millions of people five years from now.

Every day another company emerges to deliver cobbled-together insights and information from a variety of places comprising the

> ## From our interview with James Young, Vice President of Products, Spreadfast
>
> Q: What does the future of monitoring the web look like? If I asked you to look five years in the future what would it look like?
>
> A: Right now, listening is in its infancy as far as sophistication goes. We are just now starting to move beyond passive listening to really understanding the who, what, and why of the thing being said. In our face-to-face lives, we can pick up on a lot of these clues by what

we know about the person we're talking with, what we hear in their voice, and what we see in their body language.

I think the future will bring vast improvements to the algorithms detecting the true sentiment of the message so that our computers will also recognize the nuances of speech that our brains can pick up. I think the consolidation of our online personas will be complete so that we can easily access a fully fleshed-out biography of the person behind the content.

I think a counteracting force to the above is that the amount of video content will be much higher than it is now, so that we are better able to utilize our God-given deduction talents, and won't need the technology as much.

greater chatter that takes place on the Web. Most of these services evaluate Twitter content, blogs, and articles. They create a holistic view of what people are saying about your organization or cause online. In some cases, they're able to automatically determine the sentiment of the post by searching for positive and negative words in the posts. Here are three such examples of these services.

1. Cision: http://us.cision.com/media-monitoring/media-monitoring-overview.asp
2. Radian6: www.radian6.com/community/giving-back/
3. Vocus: www.vocus.com/content/pranalytics.asp

Outside of contracting with one of these three companies to monitor mentions of your NPO, what else can a nonprofit of the future do? There are hundreds of blog posts, news articles, videos, tweets, photos, and more out there every day about your organization, so how do you monitor these and use them as opportunities to move your mission?

If you are new to monitoring and want to get started with a free solution, we do have a suggestion. When David was at the American Cancer Society he used a great iGoogle Dashboard (we got the idea from Carie Lewis of the Humane Society of the United States) that he set up with numerous RSS feeds that delivered streams of content into one place for him to view and monitor. This solution may not provide you with the deepest dive, or the most comprehensive insights, but it will give you a free tool to get started with. Learn from using it and in time you will want to invest in a more complete system. Remember, the value is not in *having the data*, but in what you do with the data once you have it.

How to Get Started with Web Monitoring   This is a quick and dirty first step to get started monitoring. First make sure you have a Google account. Sign into iGoogle and begin by doing a Twitter search at https://search.twitter.com/ for your organization's name. When you do this you will get the RSS feed of the search to copy and paste as a widget in iGoogle. Repeat these steps for each key search term that you think is important to your organization.

Next, do a news search on Google News for the same terms, grab the RSS feeds and add them as widgets in iGoogle. As you begin to create and add feeds, remember to keep them organized and categorized because the data is no good if you cannot find it.

Some examples of search forums we used include:

Google News
Google blog alerts to our Gmail
DIGG RSS searches
Forum searches
Twitter searches (on a ton of different keywords)
BlogPulse searches
Flickr keyword searches

Once you have established your feeds (see Figure 10.2) you can begin to really listen to the conversations that are taking place all around you on the Web. This enables you to have the opportunity to join in and help influence discussions and opinions as a natural part of the discourse. The future of communications is partly based on knowing what to listen to and being prepared to hear the messages when they are expressed.

Trend #3: Data, Data, Data or Segmentation: Do You Even Know the Value of What You Have There?

Without a doubt the democratizing power of the Web has created a near-free public platform. There is unprecedented parity on the Web and the playing field continues to level as more powerful free

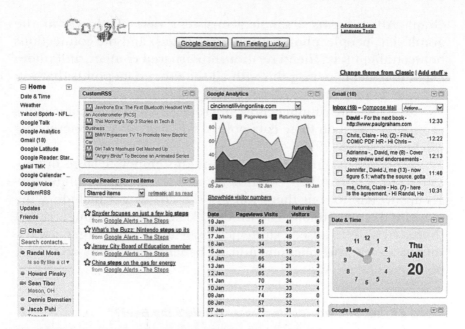

Figure 10.2   Social Media Monitoring Dashboard

tools permeate it. This phenomenon is another game changer in the nonprofit space. The open sharing of the people drawn to this medium is another boon to the nonprofit sector when it comes to communications.

In the years through 2016 and beyond, nonprofits will literally have access to thousands of data points in Constituent Relationship Management systems such as SalesForce, Razor's Edge, Convio's Common Ground, or Civi CRM. These could range from traditional metrics such as number of people in household to sex of donor to average annual gift and go all the way to nontraditional data points such as location-based check-ins (via location-based games) to minutes spent on social games (recorded by the games themselves) to travel plans (provided and shared by systems such as Tripit).

Of course, the holy grail of segmentation and targeting will be whatever Facebook morphs into by 2016. The Facebook Social Graph already exists and is currently tracking people and the connections they have to everything they care about. The Facebook

Graph API presents a simple, consistent view of objects in the graph (i.e., people, photos, events, and pages) and the connections between them (i.e., friend relationships, shared content, and photo tags). Imagine marrying this with all the other data points that you will have in your own CRM database.

Then imagine running entire micro segmented communications campaigns based on these data points. This type of cross-referencing will be a reality in 2016.

Web-based technology will continue to empower large organizations to segment their constituents and create some unique subgroups to talk to, but there will also be challenges including the increase of competition. The thing to keep in mind though is that there will also be unseen strategic opportunities for larger organizations to use this phenomenon to benefit themselves and drive pertinent and relevant content.

Trend #4: Advertising: Moving Past "Where's the Beef?"

As we get closer to 2016 and beyond, there will be a definite change in the demographics of your NPO's constituents, donors, and users. Much of this change is documented in the book *Born Digital* by John Palfrey and Urs Gasser, which we mentioned earlier. The fundamental question is which organizations will make the most of the change and prosper, and which will be late adopters and lag behind. Technology will only drive part of the solution. Organizations will need to be culturally primed to leverage opportunities as they arise. They must be ready in all three components most important to an innovation strategy: awareness, staffing, and structure.

We have been lucky enough to have heard presentations from some of the leading minds in digital media and advertising over the years. We heard author Dan Pallotta speak in 2010 at the Texas Nonprofit Summit hosted by the OneStar Foundation and Greenlights in Austin, Texas, we also saw him talk at the American Marketing Association's Nonprofit Conference that same year. For those of you that have read his book, *Uncharitable*, Pallotta's thesis is that human beings are innately charitable and that we have a desire to help our fellow man. He goes on to describe that the current system of charity we use is a bureaucracy set up to fulfill our need to help one another, and that this system has remained unexamined because doing "good" has always been good enough. Of course, though, this is changing. Pallotta goes on to criticize the nonprofit industry's advertising practices. We agree with Pallotta 100 percent and have been thinking about this mental lapse by nonprofits since we began working in the field.

As we have presented throughout this book, awareness as we know it is all but dead and advertising *with a call to action* is truly the future: "To mount a campaign to convert six billion people to love—which is essentially the role of charity—takes a lot of money... Raise the capital to promote the idea by offering a return on investment, hire the best people to manage the effort, and run the advertising to spread the word. You beat capitalism at its own game," says Pallotta.

Another way to look at this is by examining how successful the American Cancer Society's "More Birthdays Campaign" has been. According to the *New York Times*:

> "The American Cancer Society spends about $15 million a year on ads. Unlike many other nonprofit organizations, which rely on media companies to run their campaigns on a pro bono basis, it has a marketing budget to insure its pitches get more prominent display than is typically the case when campaigns appear in donated commercial time and ad space.
>
> "Paying for the ads to appear also helps the American Cancer Society better reach the target audience for its messages, which is primarily women ages 35 to 64, who are the health care decision-makers for their families.
>
> "'We have the challenge to blow the dust off a brand that will be 100 years old in 2013,' says Greg Donaldson, national vice president for corporate communications at the American Cancer Society in Atlanta."[9]

It is clear: Nonprofits need to get over the fact that budget is going to go to advertising. And donors need to get over it, as well. If we all come together as a sector to educate donors through the

---

[9]http://www.nytimes.com/2010/09/20/business/media/20adnewsletter1.html?ref=stuart_elliott

next five to ten years we will see this change start to take shape and happen. Nonprofits need advertising just like nonprofits need overhead positions like communications and accounting. Take the case of Narissa Johnson, on the communications staff of Southwest Key in Austin, Texas, who said, "I'm Overhead and Proud of It."[10] In the successful nonprofit of the future, things that were usually seen as overhead in terms of marketing and advertising are going to make a real difference, so the old mentality needs to change.

Nancy Schwartz, publisher of The Getting Attention Blog, has a good formula for how nonprofits should advertise and budget for that advertising. Here is a sample budget for you to ponder as you adjust your plans starting in 2012 for 2016.[11]

2%	Purchasing all advertising and promotion media, including Internet, newspaper, radio, TV, and direct mail (postage).
+	
4%	Producing (design, artwork) and printing all communications. This includes newsletters, brochures, websites, press kits, and so on.
+	
1.5%	Producing special events.
+	
3.5%	Salaries, consultants, and freelancers.
=	
11%	Total percentage of the organizational budget going to marketing and communications.

This is a highly-simplified example of a budget shaped by the percentage approach. The average allocation is from 9 to 12 percent of your annual organizational budget (start with 10 percent). Advocacy organizations tend to allocate a higher percentage (12 percent or higher) of their organizational budgets to communications, since much of their advocacy work is communications-based.

But don't settle on this. See how far you can push your staff and board of directors to make it happen. Most of all, measure the

---

[10]http://twitter.com/NarissaTweets/statuses/25422838917
[11]http://gettingattention.org/articles/195/planning-budgets/nonprofit-marketing-budget.html

return on your advertising spending. Set good-quality metrics that you can measure. It can be dollars generated, households touched, or even an increase in overall awareness of your organization or cause. In measuring your investment, you make it easier to optimize your efforts in the future and show your donors, executives, and constituent base that you are spending their money in the best interest of the mission.

Trend #5: The Total Loss of Privacy: The New Reality Needs a New Methodology

For better or for worse in the years through 2016 and beyond, the notion of privacy will be just that, a notion.

The wide-open nature of the Internet has created a fantastic ecosystem where individuals are allowed to roam, freely looking at websites, reading articles, and conducting their businesses. So far, we have all participated while retaining a certain sense of security and anonymity. As the Internet matures, though, privacy and anonymity will become key issues driven by a few unsavory trends: theft, terrorism, and bullying. Online theft, digital terrorism, and cyber-bullying will become rampant in the media, appearing predictably in every evening newscast and in newspaper headlines.

We have read that the government is going to move forward on a strategy that, "seeks the creation of a system for identity management that would allow citizens to use additional authentication techniques, such as physical tokens or modules on mobile phones, to verify who they are."[12] We think this may impact industries in major ways, so that individuals would lose the ability to freely roam the net without the concern that every move they are making is being watched by someone. For organizations that work in very sensitive arenas such as health, political asylum, sexual assault, and those involved in youth issues, you might begin to understand how devastating such restrictions could be. At the same time, we as users will continue the trend of publishing almost everything that we do during the course of a day online for the world to see. As smartphones advance, mobile social software and geolocation will auto report our experiences—where we go and how long we are there.

---

[12]http://www.ft.com/cms/s/2/f416e31e-80af-11df-be5a-00144feabdc0.html

It will be possible to see not just when we check in, but when we check out because, as a business, I not only want to know when you check in but also when you check out.

In the future, we will also have an expectation of our friends and family to share mass volumes of mundane details and we, in turn, will be expected to reciprocate. The trends will provide great opportunities for nonprofits to further engage their constituents in sharing every interaction, every micro donation, and every advocacy email they send within their networks. If you continue to imagine future scenarios based on the capabilities we talked about in the previous examples, including what is currently happening and just on the cusp of exploding, you can see the opportunities multiply. While Internet and technology users may end up giving up more and more of their privacy, the social media, app, and network advocates and supporters of the future will at least have a larger number of people tuned into their message. For nonprofits, as we've mentioned before, the challenge will be to provide the safest level of engagement opportunities so that their causal donors can easily take the next step and become active advocates.

Interview: The *Evil Bloggers* of 2009—Monitored and Dealt With

Part of the challenge with online space is that there is ever-shrinking privacy online. This means we need to rededicate our organizations to providing great digital experiences for our constituents. In our interview with Wendy Harman, Social Media Director of Red Cross USA, you can hear how the Red Cross has been hard at work trying to drive innovations that create exceptional constituent experiences.

David and Randy: How and what innovations did you start at your current or past job?

Wendy: I'd say the most marked innovation I've been a part of is the one your book is probably about—a shift in organizational culture driven by technology. The social Web has given an important role to our stakeholders and we've innovated to embrace that role instead of ignoring, squishing, or otherwise trying to control it. We haven't changed our mission, but we're recognizing that technology makes it easier for us to achieve our goals—to connect people and communities to help one another in emergencies.

David and Randy: How was the innovation effort initiated?

Wendy: We started from a reactive place in late 2006. It was a year after Hurricane Katrina and I was hired to make the *evil bloggers* stop saying bad things. The truth is that there weren't *evil bloggers*—there were a handful of people who cared a lot about what they saw as holes in our capacity. There were thousands of other people who were just plain passionate, positive, and looking for a way to get involved. I immediately recognized an opportunity to embrace these people and…here we are.

David and Randy: Do you have executive support for your efforts?

Wendy: Yes! I'm so lucky to have supportive bosses in Laura Howe, Roger Lowe, and Suzy DeFrancis. We're all lucky to have our President and CEO Gail McGovern leading us during this time. She's forward thinking, open to change, and enthusiastic.

David and Randy: How is your role/department structured? Does it give you more freedom to experiment with new ideas and concepts?

Wendy: I'm part of the communications department. My title is Social Media Director. I'm so lucky to have quite a bit of freedom. For example, when my heart was broken after the Haiti earthquake because so many people were using Twitter and Facebook to ask us to rescue their family members, I was given the freedom to explore how we might innovate to respond to these requests. We will never be a first-responder organization but we have been able to convene emergency

	managers and social experts to begin to discuss how to meet public expectation around getting help in emergency situations.
David and Randy:	Where/how do you generate the new ideas and concepts to test?
Wendy:	Everything I do is informed by listening and talking with the 1000+ people every day who take time to write or record their thoughts about our mission.
David and Randy:	What is your success/failure rate?
Wendy:	I don't have a chart or anything. People ask me all the time how I got the American Red Cross to allow me to do such out-of-control things. My answer is that since we started playing in the social/community space a million bajillion good things have happened and not one bad thing has happened. Now, I'm still often surprised at the reactions to our status updates on Facebook and our blog posts. Items I think will be fully embraced turn into debates and items I think are boring can get "liked" a million times. This is all a learning experiment, so I listen, learn, and adapt every day. But the big picture is a big success.
David and Randy:	What is the most valuable thing you have learned both tactically and strategically?
Wendy:	To listen. To recognize it's not about us. I mean that in this culture the focus is not on our organization but on individual people power, and our job is to be an effective liaison so that regular people can perform extraordinary acts in the face of emergency situations.
David and Randy:	Can you give us an example of a time when your organization initiated and launched a truly innovative project?
Wendy:	I think our Emergency Social Data project is innovative. We are in the process of connecting

	government (Fed, state, local, international), citizens, NPOs, and social and technology companies around figuring out ways to become more efficient at disaster response using the tools the public is already using such as Facebook and Twitter.
David and Randy:	What were the obstacles and opportunities discovered in the development process?
Wendy:	This is tricky business! There are so many people who have to agree on common solutions for us to move forward. I've been humbled by how enthusiastic all the parties are in looking for the opportunities here, but that doesn't mean there aren't challenges. It's easy to talk about this issue but not so easy to take substantive steps forward. I hope by the time your book is published that we'll have made some strides. I know internally at the Red Cross we're working diligently on how to connect the data our social volunteers collect with our time-honored disaster-response expertise so we have an even clearer situational awareness. We want information—the public has to inform how we respond.
David and Randy:	What have you learned from the experience and how has that directly translated into a better organization?
Wendy:	I think we're truly doing our jobs. We're connectors and conveners and we've recognized this gap between what the public expects and what most emergency managers can do. Both sides will have to give a little, but just getting all the parties together to acknowledge the gap and the opportunities to be better is a success. It's inspiring to see hundreds of people check their egos at the door and work together toward saving lives.
David and Randy:	Was there a formal process involved? If not, would it have been more helpful to have one?

Wendy:	Ha. I'm personally a little process-averse but work in a place that couldn't love process more. It started because we were listening. We ended up publishing a white paper and hosting a summit and now we're in the *process* of creating a *process* for taking action.
David and Randy:	Who was responsible for the original concept?
Wendy:	The public and their love for the social web.

Conclusion

The bottom line is that the way we communicate is changing at such a rapid pace that it is impacting every nonprofit's ability to conduct its business on a daily basis. Conventional wisdom is that we can either stay current with the technology by directing funds away from mission-related activities, or we keep our heads down and hope that what we have will hold us for just one more year.

But these aren't the only two solutions. There is a third way: Use the three elements of innovation (awareness, staffing, and structure) to move your organization into a position to succeed in the long run. If you take advantage of the knowledge we have provided you in this book and apply it correctly, you can create a powerful engine of new ideas and actual projects and programs. By leveraging what you have just learned, you can drive a real and meaningful change in the way that your nonprofit does business and you can watch the effects impact your staff, volunteers, constituents, and mission.

This is the point where you take the first step to making innovation happen in your organization: commitment. Coming up, we give some parting advice and timelines in Chapter 11 that will help you gauge how long of a journey you are embarking on and the last points you will need to adhere to in order to succeed.

Are you ready?

CHAPTER 11

In Conclusion

In life you will be admired for your ideas, but ultimately judged by your actions and results.

—Frank B. Moss, DDS

Y ou have finished the book. Congratulations. But this is just the beginning of your journey. You still have a long way to go and the reality is that the hardest work lies ahead of you. What we hope is that you will take what you learned from this book and begin to implement it. Starting now.

Today, Tomorrow, and Next Month

Tomorrow there is a reasonably good chance that you are going to get up in the morning, grab breakfast, and go to work. You now have this wealth of knowledge floating around in your head and you may not know how to actually get innovation going. Relax. This is a long and laborious process and it would be disingenuous if we said otherwise. To get a real and meaningful innovation program started you need to be methodical and patient, understand your organization's current state, and set realistic goals to work toward over a period of time.

You can begin by reviewing this book's appendices and taking time to not only take the quizzes and do the worksheets, but to also think critically about your organization as it stands right now. We would also love for you to join us at www.thefutureofnonprofits.com and then join our Facebook community. We will be very happy to discuss and answer questions around getting this process started. We can also guarantee that there will be others there starting on the same path.

Be meticulous in cataloging and sharing your shortcomings and the points where you can make immediate improvements and changes. Document the shortcomings and also create solutions for those shortcomings. The most important thing that you can then do is rereview the book for examples of organizations that tackled the same problems and learn from their solutions. And to be honest— no one likes to hear what is broken unless there is a solution that comes with it.

If you think that you will be able to identify all the challenges and growth opportunities in a day, you're being ambitious and missing the point. What you are doing is starting to become aware. By opening your eyes and documenting challenges you are taking the first step toward being an innovator—you are listening. And the fact that you are finding challenges means that your organization is not listening, or not able to solve the problems they are finding.

In either case, you are now better prepared to solve both of these challenges. You know how to drive awareness. You know the fundamentals of a great awareness program and know that it is the first step. Consider the various pieces of information that your organization has at its disposal and what you are, and are not, doing with it. Then look at the gaps and find sources to fill them! Make a real meaningful proposal that you can give to your director, vice president, or chief executive officer. Ensure that you have taken into account the costs and time, and be sure to explain the value to you, your management, your constituents, and the organization as whole.

Next Quarter

Since you made your case for awareness, now you need to make your case for a structural change. This is going to be the toughest challenge of all. Structural changes happen at the top and those are the people you are going to need to access for approval. Go back to the introduction and reread it. Remember how we positioned innovation and the value it drives to each of your executives? We do, and we think you should refresh yourselves on those finer points.

Before trying to sell a comprehensive structure, complete with a special work-team and special access office space, set forth a staged growth approach. Define your medium- and longer-term goals in innovation development terms: Volume of ideas you will review, white papers you will deliver, hours of consulting you will provide to internal departments, prototypes you will launch. Be aware that you are setting yourself up to be judged and measured by the outcome goals you define. Be careful and judicious in how you position your time and your achievement goals.

As you gain support in your efforts, take the time to define with precision the value that you can and will deliver to each department you interact with. In the first part of this book we talked about how innovation efforts directly impact and benefit the efforts of your executive team. Reread those first chapters now so that you can set tangible goals and show real potential value that will make their lives, and work easier.

Your efforts in developing an innovation program are similar to developing a fine wine—it takes time and patience and lot of care. Make sure that your sponsoring executives understand that in your sales process. It will take time, their patience, and your hard work to attract enough awareness information and idea submissions to begin generating solutions they can see and evaluate.

This quarter you need to focus on selling the real potential benefits of innovation and setting yourself up for future success.

Going Forward

You will soon find out that your dedication and efforts will only increase the work load! You were warned! Success begets success and as you launch and deliver innovation you will attract attention around the organization. As you refine and expand your awareness channels, strengthen your structure, and improve your staffing, you will also attract infinitely more attention.

Understand that it is paramount that you maintain focus on developing and delivering the highest quality projects that are most relevant to your constituents. A pitfall that is easy to fall into is putting development efforts behind everything that comes through your channels. Maintaining focus and being discretionary in how you spend your resources will help you maintain a consistent stream of projects and papers of the highest quality out of your innovation program.

In innovation development, complacency is the beginning of the end. Take every opportunity you can to reexamine your process to make sure that you are staying effective and relevant. Remember that even through you are the innovation center, you still need to focus energy inward to ensure that your awareness mechanisms, structure, and staff are on the leading edge. Keeping yourself current is one way that you can keep yourself relevant within your own organization. Also keeping the staff of the innovation process fresh and new is essential. Think of new people that can rotate in every two years to help advise on projects.

Understand that as your program grows and begins to impact the organization's culture as a whole, there will be people that refuse to see the value that you bring and might even make efforts to end your program for one reason or another. Prepare for that conversation every day by always showing the end value that your innovation programs are generating. Calculate the total dollars your innovation fundraising programs have raised, the new donor names you have contributed to the master database, the policies you have influenced, and the lives you have saved. Use your own organization's yardsticks to measure your contribution to the overall mission.

Understand how other departments calculate value and use those calculations to help keep your value argument grounded and give you even footing when you make the value-contribution argument.

Most of All, Enjoy It

Above all else innovation work is fun, exciting, and challenging. Do not forget that you are actively creating an intellectual sandbox for others to play in. The ideas that you develop and the ideas that you cultivate are the future of your organization. That is something to take extreme pride in, and respect simultaneously. The opportunity that you should strive to carve out within your organization is one that, ultimately, is about new projects that will substantially impact the success of your organization for years to come.

We wanted to leave you with this as our final thought: Innovation is fun. It is a lot of fun. It is exhilarating, fast-paced, and rapid work. You will be able to show a strong business return to your organization, create new ways to solve constituent challenges, and keep your employees excited about your mission. It will be frustrating at times and maddening at others but, ultimately, it is extremely rewarding work.

Innovation uncovers challenges daily and races to find answers, only to unearth two new challenges along the way. Innovation is all about listening and exploring, and as a career, it is tremendously rewarding. We challenge you to immerse yourself in this way of doing business, focusing on innovation, and hope that you have the same positive experience that we do.

APPENDICES

Sample Job Descriptions

Here you will find a few descriptions that might come in handy when you are trying to figure out what type of characteristics you need to be screening for when you are hiring innovative new team members. David used the basics from this appendix to find the perfect innovative team members for Lights. Camera. Help. These descriptions are also available by signing up for our mailing list online by joining the community at www.thefutureofnonprofits.com.

The community manager intern at Lights. Camera. Help. would hold a position with duties that combine marketing with social media to drive mission. It is a great hybrid job in a rapidly developing career field and a chance to work in a burgeoning area that is not routinely taught in college.

The manager of digital marketing innovations would hold a position with duties that combine marketing with innovations to drive mission. It is a great hybrid job when a company can't afford a full-time innovations-only manager.

Job Description: Community Manager Intern

Lights. Camera. Help. Community Manager Internship

Lights. Camera. Help. is a nonprofit organization that is dedicated to encouraging other nonprofit and cause-driven organizations to use film and video to tell their stories. We do this through education, volunteer match programs, and an annual film festival.

We are looking for interns to help fulfill the organization's mission while learning the nuts and bolts of nonprofit arts administration. While interning at Lights. Camera. Help. you will also see the inner-workings of the film industry and support the nonprofit and cause-driven film communities.

To apply for an internship with Lights. Camera. Help. please submit an email cover letter, and include a copy of your most up-to-date resume. Email us at contact@lightscamerahelp.org with all materials.

Duties include:

Writing and social media work

Editing proposals and contracts

Working with volunteers

Fundraising

Bookkeeping of tasks, projects, contractors, and client affairs

Extensive market research, trend watching, and email development

Helping to provide QA (quality assurance) for Web projects, database, and programs

Other professional tasks, as required

Everything we do happens through the Internet. You should be very comfortable and adept at using social networking sites, Web browsers, Excel (or a spreadsheet program of your choice), and be able to roll with the punches.

Passion for nonprofits and film/video is a requirement.

You should be responsible, and a clear and effective communicator on the phone, email, chat, and in person. You need to be able to work unsupervised and have your own work environment, as well as occasionally meet in central Austin to discuss tasks and projects.

Can be for class credit or volunteer hours.

Job Description: Manager of Digital Marketing Innovations

Department: Nonprofit marketing

Type: Full-time

Description of your nonprofit:

Summary:

Leading [*enter location here*]-based nonprofit seeks talented manager for our innovation team, which develops marketing and digital breakthroughs that help our constituents and staff navigate the emerging media and evolving technology landscape. Will take marketing our mission and events to the next level by embracing emerging trends and technologies to reach our mission and revenue goals in revolutionary ways. This is a special division created specifically to keep our organization current on the latest developments in technology, media, marketing, consumer behaviors, trends in popular culture, and the digital world as well as encourage, manage, and structure internal innovations within the organization.

[*Enter more about your nonprofit's mission here.*]

We are looking for a creative marketing manager to develop and execute ideas as well as present to existing and new staff and volunteers what is going on in digital media, fundraising, traditional media, and branded entertainment.

Essential responsibilities:

- Stay up-to-date on trends in technology, culture, and advertising, and be able to translate trends into new opportunities for organizational growth across all marketing platforms including print, outdoor, TV, events, social media, and digital opportunities.
- Lead and participate in innovations brainstorming sessions daily for mission specific campaigns, programs, and events.
- Assist the group in coordinating with internal departments for investigation and assessment of emerging technologies, ideas, and platforms.
- Develop relationships with vendors and source new leads in emerging media platforms.
- Manage new media campaigns from ideation to completion through entire cycle.
- Prepare and deliver presentations, both internally and externally, around mission-specific and program-specific innovations, ideation, trends, opportunities, and strategy in the area of digital media and emerging technologies.

- Support the organization in its outreach programs to academic institutions, the grant making and venture capital community, and research and development hubs as well as relevant industry forums, groups, and associations.

Job specifications:

- Successful candidates will have 3+ years in nonprofit advertising, media, or digital media background, and have an entrepreneurial spirit, yet also work well in a corporate environment.
- Must have extensive knowledge of the emerging technologies and existing media and be able to develop creative uses to help our communications "break through the clutter."
- Must have strong presentation skills and be able to generate ideas.
- Must be a person who is passionate about innovation and delivers that passion in all areas of ideation and execution.
- Advertising/marketing industry knowledge is preferred but not required.

The preceding job description documents the general nature and level of work but is not intended to be a comprehensive list of all activities, duties, and responsibilities required of job incumbents. Consequently, job incumbents may be asked to perform other duties as required.

2

Organization Innovation Index Quiz

This quiz is also available online by signing up for our mailing list at www.thefutureofnonprofits.com or by joining our digital community there.

■ ■ ■

Take this quiz and answer the questions as honestly as possible. Remember, the idea is for you to attain an idea of how innovative your organization is right now, not what your organization aspires to be. The questions are not graded; instead, they are designed to get you thinking about the difference between what you do and what you could do.

1. Think about the last small project or program that your organization launched.
   A. Can you name the individual that came up with the core idea?
   B. Do you know who was on the team that helped to develop it, if there was a team at all?
   C. The department that is now running that program, how often do they launch new programs?
   D. What kind of publicity did they give the project or program and the person who initiated the idea?
2. On your way to work this morning you had an amazing idea, something that is really unique and will change the way your

organization does business. Assuming that you want to see this idea launched:

A. Does your organization have a procedure for taking in brilliant ideas like yours? Circle One: Yes or No.

   i. If it does, do you know who to talk to about your idea? Circle One.

     a. Your direct manager/director

     b. A suggestion box

     c. An outside consultant

     d. A formal/informal committee or work group

     e. Something else we have not thought about

   ii. If it does not, have you ever wondered why?

3. If your organization has some kind of a process, what do you know about it? Answer the questions below.

A. Do you know the steps and processes that ideas go through on their way to a full-fledged program?

B. Do you know what the criteria are for success in this process?

C. Have you seen successful programs come out of this process?

D. How long does it take to get an idea through this process?

E. Does the innovation program route ideas through the same internal approval committees that other new projects go through?

F. What kind of business development coaching support does the process offer you and your amazing idea?

4. Now think about your own department and its ability to generate and launch ideas. Answer the questions below.

A. Is idea creation a component of your annual evaluations for staff?

B. When you bring up ideas to your manager or director are you told to leave that kind of thinking up to more senior leaders?

C. Does your department do brainstorming exercises that generate both business challenges and potential solutions to those challenges?

D. When you and your department come up with a solution to a problem do they have the resources (human, financial, organization, technical) to actually test and implement them?

E. More importantly does your vice president/director/ manager have the authority to initiate new project development—or do they need to attain permission from various committees and oversight boards?

5. If and when your brilliant idea gets recognition, what recognition do you receive? Circle all that apply.

   A. Are you asked to participate in the development, launch, and management of the program that came out of your idea?

   B. Will you be given public recognition of your contribution at an annual meeting or quarterly event, or even the company newsletter/website update?

   C. Are you only going to get the most value out of using the experience on your resume when you apply for your next job?

   D. If you did not get recognition for the idea and work, who did, and did they really deserve it?

6. If you answered YES to C or D in the last question ask yourself why.

   A. Is there simply a lack of a culture of entrepreneurial spirit?

   B. Do you feel that good work is rewarded and good ideas are not?

   C. Do you see too many great ideas not being developed because of organizational barriers and ineptitude?

   D. Do you feel that because your personal success is not tied to the success of your idea that the program is treated as more important/valuable than you?

Now you have a baseline for understanding some fundamental truths about the current state of your organization's innovation capacity. This questionnaire was really designed to help you assess a few key factors of the innovation process:

- The existence of a functional structure for innovation development,
- The willingness of the organization to seek out and act on innovative ideas,
- The encouragement and support they provide their employees,

- The level to which they encourage and reward employees for their contribution, and
- How well they make the value of the innovation program apparent to their staff.

Use what you learned about your organization here to set levels. Initiating an innovation program is much easier when you understand where your starting point is. Moving forward, make sure that you keep all of these questions in mind so that you create the most effective innovation program possible. A program that is efficient, honestly engages, and recognizes and rewards the innovators is bound to be a success. Talk to others about this quiz at www.thefutureofnonprofits.com in our Community section.

APPENDIX

Are You Looking to the Future?

We cannot emphasize enough that part of being innovative and opportunistic in any business is being prepared for the future. A substantial part of your organization's success is going to rely on your ability to look forward into the future. So the questions below are designed to help you assess how well you are looking to the future.

■ ■ ■

1. What was the last conference that you attended that was not a company-sponsored retreat, regional meeting, or national summit?

2. Your colleagues travel to conferences, right? So when was the last time you saw their notes? Or the blog posts they wrote about the sessions they participated in?

3. Does your organization make a habit of passing around articles from nonindustry publications that pertain to macro trends in economics, society, and demographics?

4. What are the restrictions on your Internet browsing? Honestly—if you cannot access external sites that have valuable future-thinking information can you really be expected to know what is going on outside of your organization?

5. Do you know if your organization has an active group that is dedicated to scanning the outside environment for future opportunities?

6. If you do not know how to answer question five, do you know who you would ask to find out?

7. When was the last time your organization conducted a comprehensive survey of your donors and your constituents to understand their needs and the macro trends that are impacting their lives?

8. Walk around your office and look at the magazines that are on the desks and conference tables. Those titles say something about your organization. What are they saying to you?

9. Regardless of your job, do you know the five macro trends that can impact your organization's mission? (Federal health research spending, local legislative initiatives, ecological changes in the South East Asian wetlands, etc.) Do you know two macro trends that can impact those macro trends? Does anyone in your organization?

■ ■ ■

There are no right or wrong answers. Realizing that your organization is or is not paying attention to the things that could impact it most is a startling discovery. The world is large and complex and being aware of the big picture and sharing that knowledge can actually help you focus on the little picture.

If you are not thinking about the future, you are destined to become a thing of the past.

Index